Life After Death

A Study of the Afterlife in World Religions

FARNÁZ MA'SÚMIÁN

ONEWORLD
OXFORD

Dedicated to the memory of my beloved father, Mr. Abbás Shaykhzádeh,
and to my dear teachers,
who sacrificed their lives to promote the cause of
love and the unity of humankind:

– DR. ALIMURÁD DÁVUDÍ
– MR. MUHAMMAD MUVAHHID
– MR. BADI'U'LLÁH FARÍD

Life After Death

Oneworld Publications
(Sales and Editorial)
185 Banbury Road
Oxford OX2 7AR
England

Oneworld Publications
(US Marketing Office)
PO Box 830, 21 Broadway
Rockport, MA 01966
USA

© Farnáz Ma'súmián 1995
Reprinted 1996

ISBN 1–85168–074–8

Printed and bound by
WSOY, Finland

CONTENTS

ACKNOWLEDGMENTS

I am indebted to many individuals and institutions for their assistance in bringing this book to fruition. First, I would like to thank my very talented friend Trey Yancy, graphic artist and senior editor of *Deepen* magazine, who spent many hours of his valuable time drawing two of the illustrations (nos. 2 and 3). I also want to thank my good friend and colleague Dr. Robert Stockman, Professor of World Religions at Depaul University, for reviewing a copy of the manuscript and offering many useful suggestions.

Next I am grateful to my dear husband Bijan Ma'súmián, without whose support, encouragement, and assistance what was originally a Master's thesis could not have been turned into this book. He not only reviewed the manuscript but made major contributions to the last two chapters, researched and obtained the artwork, and worked closely with Trey Yancy in the design work.

Finally I would like to give heartfelt thanks to the individuals, museums, and art galleries listed below who provided me with artworks at little or no charge:

Dr. Wibke Lobo, Museum für Indische Kunst, Berlin, Germany (Illustrations 1, 5); Kunsthistorisches Museum, Vienna, Austria (Illustration 4); Mary L. Sluskonis, Museum of Fine Arts, Boston, Massachusetts, USA (Illustration 8); Palazzo Ducale, Venice, Italy (Illustration 9); Geneviève Bonté, Bibliothèque des Arts Décoratifs, Paris, France (Illustration 10).

Material from *The Light Beyond*, © 1988 by Dr. Raymond A. Moody, Jr., is used by permission of Bantam Books, a division of Bantam Doubleday Dell Publishing Group, Inc.

Excerpts from *Life After Life*, © 1975 by Dr. Raymond A. Moody, Jr., are used by permission of MBB, Inc.

PREFACE

A man is dying and, as he reaches the point of greatest physical distress, he hears himself pronounced dead by his doctor. He begins to hear an uncomfortable noise, a loud ringing or buzzing, and at the same time feels himself moving very rapidly through a long dark tunnel. After this, he suddenly finds himself outside his own physical body, but still in the immediate environment, and he sees his own body from a distance, as though he is a spectator. He watches the resuscitation attempt from this unusual vantage point and is in a state of emotional upheaval.

After a while, he collects himself and becomes accustomed to his odd condition. He notices that he still has a 'body' but one of a very different nature and with very different powers from the physical body he has left behind. Soon other things begin to happen. Others come to meet and help him. He glimpses the spirits of relatives and friends who have already died, and a loving, warm spirit of a kind he has never encountered before – a being of light – appears before him. This being asks him a question, nonverbally, to make him evaluate his life and helps him along by showing him a panoramic, instantaneous playback of the major events of his life. At some point, he finds himself approaching some sort of barrier or border, apparently the limit between earthly life and the next life. Yet, he finds that he must go back to the earth, that the time for his death has not yet come.

At this point, he resists, for by now he is taken up with his experiences in the afterlife and does not want to return. He is overwhelmed by intense feelings of joy, love, and peace. Despite his attitude, though, he somehow reunites with his physical body and lives.[1]

Are there any parallels between the above account of a near-death experience, from Raymond Moody's classic work *Life After Life*, and what happens to us when we actually die? Is there indeed a part of us that conquers death and continues to live a different kind of existence where it has new powers and undergoes unfamiliar experiences? If so, will that entity have a personal or universal encounter with its creator at some point? Is there really a heaven, or numerous heavens, full of blissful joys awaiting some of us and a hell or countless hells full of different punishments for others? Will there ever be a general resurrection and a final judgment for all humanity? Or is physical death, in fact, the end of life as we know it? Questions about death and dying have intrigued humanity since the dawn of time. Moody's work, first published in 1975, generated a great deal of interest about the afterlife. Several books have since been published on the subject, but none have examined cross-religious perspectives and the near-death experience in a single volume.

In this book, I first provide a general overview of the death and life-after-death doctrines (eschatology) of seven world religions, mainly through their scriptures. These are the Hindu, Zoroastrian, Jewish, Buddhist, Christian, Muslim, and Bahá'í religions. Then I examine the viability of the reincarnation and transmigration theories, which offer a unique perspective on earthly existence. The last two chapters deal with the mysterious phenomenon known as the near-death experience (NDE). First I provide an overview of the NDE and the various theories that have attempted to explain this puzzling experience. Then, in the last chapter, I offer a number of remarkable parallels between the religious and NDE accounts of afterlife.

As some readers may anticipate, the afterlife doctrines of the two eastern religious traditions included here – Hinduism and Buddhism – are notably different from those of the other religions, because both Hindu and Buddhist eschatologies revolve around the intertwined doctrines of *samsara* (reincarnation or transmigration) and *karma* (you reap what you sow), which are, in a strict sense, absent from the other religious systems discussed here.

Since this book is intended as a simple introduction, no detailed descriptions or exhaustive analysis of various eschatological concepts are provided here. However, whenever appropriate, the transfer of ideas or doctrines from one religion to another has been noted.

Concern for brevity also prohibited the inclusion of denominational and sectarian belief systems. For a denominational slant, see Johnson and

McGee's *Encounters with Eternity*.[2] Here my emphasis is usually on the doctrines as found in the universally accepted scriptures of each religion. However, this was not always possible, particularly in the case of eastern religions and Judaism. Various schools of Hinduism and Buddhism have their own canonized scriptures with divergent, sometimes conflicting, views of life and death. I have deliberately risked oversimplification to make those chapters easier to grasp. In the case of Judaism, there is a dearth of afterlife accounts in canonized Jewish scriptures, so I have included relevant ideas from several popular but non-canonical Hebrew books.

To provide a contextual framework for readers who may not be familiar with certain religions or their sacred literature, I have included a brief introduction and classification of the scriptures of each religion at the beginning of each chapter. These may be found particularly helpful in the case of complex religious systems such as Hinduism and Buddhism. Also, glossaries at the ends of the chapters on the various religions provide a quick reference for important terms and concepts.

Lastly, due to the religious implications of the abbreviations BC (Before Christ) and AD (Anno Domini/In the Year of Our Lord), which are unacceptable to followers of most of the religions covered here, I have replaced these with the letters BCE (Before Common Era) and CE (Common Era) throughout this book.

I sincerely hope that the publication of this preliminary work on the afterlife, linking religious perspectives and the near-death experience, generates enthusiasm for further in-depth studies of this nature in the future.

Farnáz Ma'súmián
Spring 1995

Notes

1. R. A. Moody, Jr., *Life After Life: The Investigation of a Phenomenon – Survival of Bodily Death*, pp. 21–2

2. C. J. Johnson & M. G. McGee, *Encounters With Eternity: Religious Views of Death and Life After Death*

CHAPTER 1

HINDUISM

INTRODUCTION

Hinduism is probably the oldest religious system in the world. It is also arguably the most complex of living religions – in fact, many consider Hinduism to be a way of life rather than a distinct religion. Anything related to Hinduism defies a simple description, but it can best be defined as a collection of religious and moral ideas and practices that have been gradually linked together through successive generations. Today, there are many strands of Hinduism with diverse sacred literature, beliefs, and practices.

Unlike most belief systems, Hinduism's roots cannot be traced back to a single historical figure; numerous ancient and modern prophets, mystics, saints, and philosophers have contributed to its evolution through the ages. Many acceptable systems of Hindu philosophy exist, but most Hindus follow one of six traditional philosophies. The three most popular philosophies are:

Sankhya
A dualist view that considers matter and spirit as eternally separate realities, the Sankhya denies the existence of a creator God and is, therefore, an atheistic philosophy.

The Yoga System
This system's views regarding matter and spirit are similar to the Sankhya, but Yoga teaches the existence of a creator God and is, thus, a theistic philosophy.

The Vedanta System
This is the most popular system. There are three different views within the Vedanta system.

Non-Dualism

Non-dualists believe that the ultimate reality is Brahman (Absolute Reality or God). Brahman is considered the only true existence. All creation is merely a manifestation of Brahman in time and space. To the non-dualist, the root cause of all suffering is the soul's ignorance of its real nature, so the purpose of life is release from this suffering and union with Brahman. We can obtain this release only by understanding our true nature (self-knowledge).

Qualified Non-Dualism

Those who follow qualified non-dualism consider Brahman to be impersonal, transcendent, indescribable, and the essence of pure consciousness. In their view, at some point in history Brahman transformed Himself into a personal God (Ishvara), the universe, and all the souls. The human soul is in bondage because of its alienation from this personal God, and we can free ourselves only by attempting to communicate with God.

Dualism

Dualists also see Brahman as a personal God who is the creator of everything. However, they regard the world of creation as real but separate from Brahman and dependent on Him for its existence. They attribute the bondage of the human soul to its forgetfulness of its creator, and believe that liberation can be achieved through communion with God.

As the above definitions indicate, the unfolding of Hinduism through the ages has brought about an astonishing variety of opinion, and areas of disagreement have arisen among its adherents. However, most Hindus acknowledge the sacredness of the categories of writings described below.

SACRED LITERATURE

Shruti (that which is heard)

Vedic sacred literature, which is revered as revelation.

Vedas

The literal meaning of the term Veda is 'sacred knowledge.' Broadly, the entire body of Hindu sacred writings is known as the Vedas. In the narrower definition, the term refers to four specific books, chief among which is the Rig-Veda, an anthology of religious poetry in praise of various Hindu deities who are assumed to reside on the earth, in the intermediate air, and in the heavens. The Rig-Veda consists of ten books, containing 1,028 hymns. These hymns were collected over a span of 600 years, *circa* 1500–900 BCE. The Rig-Veda is among the most ancient religious writing to survive today.

Brahmanas

Brahmanas are a series of prose commentaries on the Vedas, written by various Hindu sages between 850 and 500 BCE. These commentaries stress the potency of Vedic rituals and sacrifices for exerting control over gods, nature, and humanity.

Upanishads

Upanishads, 'sitting near a teacher,' are a series of speculative treatises also written by Hindu sages. These writings expand on the philosophical meanings of the Vedas, and are in the form of dialogues. The Upanishads were written over a period of three to four hundred years, terminating about 300 BCE.

Smriti (that which is remembered)

Non-Vedic sacred literature, revered as tradition. This class of Hindu scriptures includes a plethora of different writings which address diverse topics ranging from grammar and etymology to medicine and hygiene, philosophy, and sectarian beliefs. Popular literature such as the Puranas (eighteen books of religious poems) and the two greatest epics of India, *Ramayana* and *Mahabharata*, fall into this category. The *Mahabharata* is the world's longest epic. It contains 220,000 lines, that is over seven times the combined length of the *Iliad* and the *Odyssey*. India's best loved devotional book, the Bhagavad Gita, is part of the *Mahabharata* epic.

PERSONAL ESCHATOLOGY

Personal eschatology is concerned with the immediate fate of righteous and unrighteous souls following death, and the conditions governing each category of souls between death and the universal resurrection of humanity. General eschatology, on the other hand, considers the final destiny of the whole human race, especially the events of the last days, that is universal resurrection and final judgment. Hinduism, however, is only concerned with *personal* eschatology.

As with any aspect of Hinduism, a consideration of its teachings about death and afterlife must take into account its various sectarian beliefs. Different philosophies of Hinduism hold divergent views about what happens when we die, but the twin doctrines of *karma* (you reap what you sow) and *samsara* (transmigration) are at the center of the eschatological beliefs of most Hindus.

According to the *samsara* (literally, 'the round of existence') doctrine, the present life of each person is shaped by the fruits of the acts he or she has performed in previous lives. *Karma* can be defined as the law of automatic justice. For every action, there is a reward or retribution; all our present pleasures, pains, and sufferings are the direct result of our past actions.

As long as our *karma* results in sins and imperfections, we will continue to be reborn into other existences. More than likely, these successive rebirths will not be on the same plane of being – they may occur in any of a number of temporary heavens or hells, or on earth. Rebirths on earth may, in turn, be in any life-form: vegetable, animal, or human. Human rebirth is considered most significant because only in human form can we accumulate good *karma*. Traditional Hindu literature such as the Puranas identify numerous temporary heavens and hells that are set aside for karmic retribution. Once the consequences of virtuous or evil deeds are exhausted, the soul is reborn as a human being on earth. The purpose of life is to break the vicious cycle of birth–death–rebirth and liberate one's soul, but very few of us can do this at any given time. The vast majority of humans fail to release themselves from the bondage of *karma* and *samsara* and are thus condemned to endless rebirths. Naturally, the twin doctrines of *samsara* and *karma* make the meaning of death and the afterlife in Hinduism very different from the views offered by most other religions.

Buddhism, however, which began as a reform movement within

Hinduism and later developed into an independent world religion, has many similarities; while most other religious systems acknowledge only one earthly experience for our souls, Hindu and Buddhist religions see them returning to earth countless times in various life forms as part of a unique system of retribution.

Interestingly, there is no reference to either the transmigration or *karma* doctrines in any of the four Vedas which are the most ancient and sacred of Hindu scriptures. These doctrines first appear in the Upanishads. In fact, the Vedas contain a number of references to a single earthly life, to be followed by an everlasting existence for the human soul on a different, non-material plane of existence.

The Rig-Veda
For example, the following passage in the Rig-Veda alludes to the existence of a single heaven as a kingdom where believers will enjoy eternal life:

> The kingdom of inexhaustible light,
> Whence is derived the radiance of the sun,
> To this kingdom transport me,
> Eternal, undying. (IX. 113:7)[1]

The Rig-Veda also contains more explicit references to heaven. It notes that the way to heaven is perilous and believers will have to face many dangers before getting there, including demons who are ready to devour them should they stray from the right path. To help the faithful in this dangerous journey, the Rig-Veda identifies a colorful god named Yama. Yama was the first man to die but is now the god of the dead and the ruler and judge of the departed. Ancient Hindus remembered Yama when addressing the spirits of their dead, whose bodies were burned on the funeral pyre:

> Honor with thine oblations the King, Yama, who gathers
> men together.
> Who traveled to the lofty heights above us, who searches
> out and shows the path to many.

Yama first found for us a place to dwell in: this pasture never
can be taken from us. (X. 14: 1–2)

To prevent the faithful from falling prey to the demons, Yama's broad-
nosed, four-eyed watchdogs are instructed to guard the path to heaven:

And those two dogs of thine, Yama, the watchers,
four-eyed, who look on men and guard the pathway.
Entrust this man, O King, to their protection, and
with prosperity and health endow him.
Dark-hued, insatiate, with distended nostrils, Yama's
two envoys roam among the people;
May they restore to us a fair existence here and today,
that we may see the sunlight. (X. 14: 11–12)

According to the Rig-Veda, heaven is the reward for such virtues as aus-
terity, making offerings and gifts to the priests, following the holy law,
and for death in battle.[2] The joys and pleasures of heaven are described in
very tangible forms; for instance, spirits are portrayed as enjoying a blissful life in a world of perpetual light, spending their time drinking *soma* (a
stimulating, exotic juice), milk, honey, and ghee and listening to the
sound of singing and flutes. There are also wish-cows that grant all the
wishes of these spirits. The companions of the inhabitants of heaven are
the forefathers of the deceased and various Hindu gods, including Yama,
humanity's first ancestor who, as mentioned above, is now the king and
judge of all the dead.[3]

Go forth, go forth upon the ancient pathways
whereon our sires of old have gone before us.
There shalt thou look on both the Kings
enjoying their sacred food,
God Varuna and Yama.
Meet Yama, meet the Fathers [dead ancestors], meet the
merit of free or ordered acts, in highest heaven.
Leave sin and evil, seek anew thy dwelling,
and bright with glory meet another body. (X. 14: 7–8)

The above passage not only mentions heaven but also states that the departed will wear "another body" – an explicit reference to a different frame for the soul. While later Hindu scriptures identify many hells, the Vedas mention only one, a deep, dark, bottomless pit where the gods Indra (god of storms and the monsoon) and Soma (god of libation) throw the wicked, including demons, sorcerers, and conspirators:

> Indra and Soma, plunge the wicked in the depth, yea, cast
> them into darkness that hath no support.
> So that not one of them may ever thence return
> So may your wrathful might prevail and conquer them.
> (VII. 104:3)

The Upanishads

As noted above, the Upanishads are commentary treatises on the four Vedas. While the main purpose of these treatises was to explain the philosophical meanings found in the Vedas, the authors of certain Upanishads introduced additional non-Vedic concepts that changed the face of Hindu beliefs and practices forever. Among these were the two influential doctrines of *samsara* and *karma*, which permanently left their marks on Hindu eschatology. The Upanishads appear to use these doctrines to justify the sufferings and injustices of human life.[4] Leaving the door of return to this earth open gave both the sinful and the unfortunate the hope of a better life in the future. Among the various Upanishads, the Brhad-áranyaka Upanishad is the first to mention the *samsara* doctrine.

The Brhad-áranyaka Upanishad

The major theme of the Brhad-áranyaka Upanishad is the concept of unity of existence or existential monism. According to this notion, all souls come forth from Brahman like sparks from the fire.[5] Therefore, only one soul exists in all beings, and all existence shares the same essence: "He [Brahman] is your soul, which is in all things" (3. 4. 1). When, through ignorance, a person fails to see this unity and considers himself separate from Brahman, he subjects himself to sorrow, fear, and successive rebirths:

> By the mind alone is It to be perceived.
> There is on earth no diversity.
> He gets death after death,
> Who perceives here seeming diversity. (4. 4. 19)

The only way one can release oneself from the vicious cycle of rebirths is to realize the essential unity of all existence. One can accomplish this by reading the Vedas and through meditation, fasting, faith, sacrifice, asceticism, and a celibate life:

> This [the self] it is which they seek to know through repetition of the Vedas, through celibate life, through asceticism, through faith, through sacrifice, and through fasting. When one knows this he becomes a Muni (silent sage). This it is which wandering ascetics seek as their heavenly worlds as they wander forth as ascetics.[6]

By recognizing the unity of existence, one obtains *moksha* (liberation or release) from desire for the world, from fear, ignorance, evil, and sorrow. Once released, one sees all souls in oneself and oneself in all souls. One becomes a lover of all beings and will have no fear of anything, nor be a cause of fear or harm to any creature:

> Therefore, having this knowledge [of unity of existence], having become calm, subdued, quiet, patiently enduring, and collected, one sees the Soul just in the soul. One sees everything as the Soul. Evil does not overcome him: He overcomes evil. Evil does not burn him: He burns all evil. Free from evil, free from impurity, free from doubt, he becomes a Brahmana.[7]

A Brahmana (a knower of Brahman) enjoys a life of peace and tranquillity while still on earth and, upon his departure from this world, obtains *moksha* and his soul (*atman*) completely merges into the Supreme Soul like a lump of salt in the ocean, never to be separated again:

All the diverse elements, in the end, go back to the soul and
are absorbed in it, as all waters are finally absorbed in the
ocean . . . A lump of salt may be produced by separating it
from the water of the ocean. But when it is dropped into the
ocean, it becomes one with the ocean and can not be separated again.[8]

Maitri Upanishad
The Maitri Upanishad also recognizes the unity of existence:

For Nature's sake and for its own
Is existence manifold in thee.
O Lord of all, hail unto thee!
The Soul of all, causing all acts,
Enjoying all, all life art thou!
Lord (prabhu) of all pleasure and delight! (5. 1)

However, according to this Upanishad, it is the human attachment to
worldly desires that leads us to forget the essential unity of our souls with
Brahman and, consequently, to subject ourselves to successive rebirths:

Objects of sound and touch and sense
Are worthless objects in a man.
Yet the elemental soul through attachment to them
Remembers not the highest place. (4. 2)

Once again, the only way to liberate oneself from *samsara* is to come to the
realization that the essence of all things is one and the same thing. In addition to various methods of release identified in the Brhad-áranyaka
Upanishad, the Maitri Upanishad prescribes a new way – the practice of
six-fold yoga. This includes controlled breathing (*Pranayama*), withdrawal
of the senses (*Pratyahara*), meditation (*Dhyana*), concentration (*Dharana*),
contemplation (*Tarka*), and absorption or complete union with the object
of meditation (*Samadhi*).

In the final stage (absorption), the true nature of the self becomes clear to the yogi and he will see no distinction between his soul and his Maker:

> When a seer sees the brilliant
> Maker, Lord, Person, the Brahma-source,
> Then, being a knower, shaking off good and evil,
> He reduces everything to unity in the supreme Imperishable.
> (6. 18)

Thus, the Brahmana is released from the cycle of rebirths and, upon death, his soul reunites with Brahman from whom it had emanated.

The Bhagavad Gita

The Bhagavad Gita (Song of the Blessed Lord) ranks among the most popular Hindu scriptures. It is one of the great classics of religious literature and has influenced Hindu thought for over 2,000 years, and particularly in the last 100 years. The Bhagavad Gita upholds the unity of existence and reincarnation presented in the Upanishads and offers three distinct paths to liberation. The first two are traditional Upanishadic methods. But the third and most favored method of release is a distinctly new path.

The Path of Knowledge (Jnana-marga)

The central figure here is Krishna, a popular Hindu god. He approves the Upanishadic suggestion of using meditation and yoga to gain insight into one's identity with Brahman:

> The man of faith gets knowledge,
> Intent solely upon it, restraining his senses.
> Having got knowledge, to supreme peace
> In no long time he goes. (4. 39)

> When the various states of beings
> He perceives as abiding in one,
> And from that alone their expansion,
> Then he attains Brahman. (13. 30)

The Path of Disinterested Action (Karma-marga)
The Bhagavad Gita also reaffirms the validity of the path of disinterested action for liberating oneself from *moksha*. Krishna teaches that what causes rebirths is not our actions but our attachment to the *rewards* of those actions. Therefore, the way to release oneself from rebirths is to perform religious and caste duties without concern for reward:

> On action alone be thy interest,
> Never on its fruits;
> Let not the fruits of action be thy motive,
> Nor be thy attachment to inaction. (2. 47)

> Perform thou action that is (religiously) required;
> For action is better than inaction.
> And even the maintenance of the body for thee
> Can not succeed without action. (3. 8)

> Therefore, unattached ever
> Perform action that must be done;
> For performing action without attachment
> Man attains the highest. (3. 19)

The Bhagavad Gita prefers the path of disinterested action to the path of knowledge because it is easier and more accessible to the unsophisticated masses.

The Path of Devotion (Bhakti-marga)
The Bhagavad Gita's favored way of salvation is a new path called the 'path of devotion.' Here, devotion means absolute dedication of one's heart and mind to Krishna, calling on His name, reciting praises of Him, and always keeping Him in mind. It means devoting one's life to the loving worship and service of Krishna without any desire for other things in life:

> Give me thy mind and give me thy heart,
> Give me thy offerings and thy adoration;

And thus with thy soul in harmony,
And making me thy goal supreme,
Thou shalt in truth come to me. (9. 34)

According to the Bhagavad Gita, the path of devotion is the easiest way
to release ourselves from successive rebirths. Thus, the simplest devotion
is more acceptable than the most complex sacrifices:

If one gives me with devotion
Leaf or flower, fruit or water,
From that earnest soul I relish
Such an offering of devotion. (9. 26)

Another advantage of the path of devotion is that, unlike the other two
paths, this path is not exclusive: it is open to both sexes, all castes, and to
righteous and unrighteous alike:

Even if a very evil-doer
Reveres Me with single devotion,
He must be regarded as righteous in spite of all;
For he has the right resolution.

Quickly his soul becomes righteous,
And he goes to eternal peace,
Son of Kunti, make sure of this:
No devotee of Mine is lost.

For all those who come to me for shelter,
However weak or humble or sinful they may be,
Women, artisans, and servants
They all reach the Path supreme. (9. 30–32)

As one of the most ancient and complex religious systems in the world, it
is not remarkable that the Hindu belief system has seen so much change
through the centuries. In fact, the distinguishing mark of Hindu eschatology might be change. While the afterlife ideas of early Hindu scriptures

are straightforward, the later eschatology of this religion evolves into one of the most complex in the world. The Rig-Veda, one of the oldest surviving religious documents, contains references to a simple afterlife system of retribution based on an eternal heaven and an eternal hell. But with the gradual introduction of more complex notions in the Upanishads, such as the unity of existence (existential monism) and transmigration, the face of Hindu eschatology began to change. Changes also came about in Hindu perspectives on earthly life and on what happens to us when we die. While in early Hindu works a clear line separated our earthly existence from our afterlife, in later Hindu literature this line has gradually been erased.

The authors of the Upanishads played a major role in this change by transforming the eternal heaven and hell of early Hinduism into an elaborate system of temporary heavens and hells where the dead received due recompense between rebirths. As a result, for most Hindus today, existence has come to mean entanglement in a seemingly never-ending cycle of births and deaths.

NOTES

1. This and the following extracts are taken from R. T. H. Griffith (trans.), *The Hymns of the Rig Veda*.

2. P. D. Mehta, *Early Indian Religious Thought*, p. 68

3. A. B. Keith, *The Religion and Philosophy of the Vedas and Upanishads*, vol. 32, p. 407

4. C. J. Bleeker. and G. Widengren, *Historia Religionum*, pp. 318–19

5. H. V. Clasenapp, *Immortality and Salvation in Indian Religions*, p. 17

6. T. Hopkins, *The Hindu Religious Tradition*, p. 48

7. R. E. Hume, *The Thirteen Principal Upanishads*, p. 144

8. S. Nikhilanada, *Essence of Hinduism*, p. 92

GLOSSARY

Atman: 'Breath.' Narrowly, the inner, transcendental self of a human being; broadly, the soul in all living things.

Bhagavad Gita: 'Song of the Blessed Lord.' Part of the *Mahabharata* epic poem, it ranks among the most popular Hindu scriptures.

Bhakti-marga: 'Path of Devotion.' The Bhagavad Gita's favored way to liberation from rebirths.

Brahman: 'Absolute Reality.' The impersonal Hindu God whose reality is shared by *atman* (human soul) in the monist Brahman–Atman equation.

Brahmanas: 'Rituals/Sacrifices to Brahman.' A series of prose commentaries on the Vedas, written by various Hindu sages.

Indra: God of storms and the monsoon.

Ishvara: Personalized form of God as contrasted with the impersonal Brahman. Hindus who practice non-qualified dualism believe that, at some point, the impersonal Brahman transformed Himself into the personal Ishvara.

Jnana-marga: 'Path of Knowledge.' An Upanishadic way to liberation from rebirths.

Karma: 'Volitional good or evil and its retribution.' The law of *karma* says you reap what you sow.

Karma-marga: 'Path of Disinterested Action.' An Upanishadic way to liberation from rebirths.

Mahabharata: 'Great Descendant of Bharata King or Tribe.' A huge Hindu epic poem which includes the Bhagavad Gita.

Moksha: 'Release.' Liberation from the cycle of *samsara* (rebirths).

Reincarnation: Rebirth into another body of the same species, particularly human.

Rig-Veda: 'Praise of Knowledge.' An anthology of religious poetry in praise of various Hindu deities residing on the earth, in the intermediate air, and in the heavens; consists of ten books, containing 1,028 hymns.

Samsara: 'Rebirth,' 'Impermanence.' A sequence of change; vicious cycle of rebirths that afflicts all living things until release (*moksha*). See reincarnation and transmigration.

Shruti: 'That which is heard.' A broad category of ancient Hindu scripture that includes the

Vedas and the Upanishads.

Smriti: 'That which is remembered.' The second major category of Hindu sacred scripture; includes non-Vedic literature such as the *Mahabharata* epic poem containing the well-loved Bhagavad Gita.

Soma: Sacred drink; also the ritual-priest god of libations.

Transmigration: Similar to but broader than reincarnation. While reincarnation refers to rebirth into another body of the same species, transmigration indicates passage across the boundaries of all forms of existence: plant, animal, human, demonic, and divine.

Unity of Existence: 'Existential Monism.' A Hindu doctrine that states that the human soul (*atman*), the universe, and Brahman are all one in essence.

Upanishads: 'Sitting Near a Teacher.' A series of speculative treatises written by Hindu sages.

Vedas: 'Sacred Knowledge.' Broadly, the entire body of Hindu sacred writings. Narrowly, four specific books, the most well-known of which is the Rig-Veda.

Yama: The first man to die, who later became the god/king/judge of the dead.

CHAPTER 2
ZOROASTRIANISM

INTRODUCTION

Zoroastrianism was the ancient r eligion of Persia (Iran) preached by Zoroaster (the Greek equivalent of the Iranian name Zarathustra, later Zardusht). No one knows exactly when Zoroaster appeared – estimates range from 1700 to 660 BCE. If the earliest date is accurate, Zoroaster would be the first prophet in the history of religions.[1]

Zoroaster believed He had seen God in visions and was chosen by Him to preach a new religion. He condemned and fought the priestly cults of His time, repudiated their gods as demons and exalted the 'heaven god' Ahuramazd (Ahura Mazda/Mazdah), the Wise Lord, as the divine power. The ancient notion of a constant battle between the forces of 'good' and 'evil' also has its roots in Zoroastrianism. According to Zoroaster, two ways of life are in conflict: the good against the evil. All beings, earthly and heavenly, are involved in this struggle; all humanity has free will and must choose a side in the battle. Those on the side of 'goodness' would manifest good thoughts, good words, and good deeds; those on the evil side would do the opposite.

Zoroaster promised a share of the glory of the final victory over evil to all those who fought on the side of the Wise Lord. The final destiny of human beings would be decided in an individual judgment after death, and at the universal judgment after resurrection. The righteous would go to heaven, the evil to hell.[2] "Zoroaster was, then, the first prophet in history to teach belief in the two judgments, heaven, hell, and the resurrection of the body."[3]

Zoroaster's teachings fascinated the great kings of the ancient Persian empire. During the Achaemenid dynasty (559–330 BCE) Zoroastrianism flourished under such rulers as Cyrus the Great, Darius I, and Xerxes, and it became the official religion of the Persian empire. When Alexander the Great conquered Persia, Greek cultural influences left their mark on this religion, but Zoroastrianism continued to dominate the religious lives of the Persians during the Parthian (250 BCE–226 CE) and Sassanian (226–651 CE) dynasties.

With the Arab invasion and conquest of Persia in 651 CE, Islam quickly displaced Zoroastrianism and became the official religion. Persecution forced many Zoroastrians to migrate to India. Today, most of the followers of this religion continue to live in Iran (formerly Persia) and India.

SACRED LITERATURE

The Avesta ('the Scriptures' or 'Wisdom/Knowledge')
The Avesta is among the great religious documents of antiquity, and contains records of one of the most ancient religions. Traditionally, all of the Avesta was believed to have been revealed to Zoroaster, but only seventeen hymns, known as the Gathas or Hymns of Zoroaster, can be attributed to Him. All of the Avesta, except the Gathas, was written in the Avestan language, an East Iranian language of the Indo-European family with close ties to Vedic, the language of the Hindu Vedas. Parts of the Avesta pre-date Zoroaster, while others date from approximately the time of Christ.

In ancient Persia, writing was considered an alien art and therefore unsuitable for sacred words. Thus for many years Avestan materials were memorized by priests. The first written compilation of the Avesta appeared around the third or fourth century of the Christian Era, but devising an accurate and comprehensive version took a few more centuries. When the Sassanian dynasty began, the Avesta was given wide currency, and Zoroastrianism became the state religion of Persia. Most of the original Avestan manuscripts were destroyed during the invasions of the Arabs (in the seventh century), the Turks (eleventh century) and the Mongols (twelfth century).[4] Only about a quarter of the original Avesta has survived these invasions.

The Zand
The Zand contained the translations of and commentaries on the Avesta. The only surviving Zand is in the Pahlavi language (Middle Persian).

Later Avestan Texts
These refer to certain texts written in the Avestan language many years after Zoroaster revealed the Gathas.

Pahlavi Literature
This is Zoroastrian sacred literature of the third to tenth centuries, written in Pahlavi. Most existing Zoroastrian texts fall into this category because the diligent recording of Zoroastrian literature began during the Sassanian dynasty, when Pahlavi was the official language of Persia.

PERSONAL ESCHATOLOGY

Zoroastrianism appears to be the oldest major religious system to contain an explicit personal and general eschatology. Zoroaster was probably the first prophet in history to speak of a universal judgment at the end of time as well as an individual judgment at death. His Gathas are the oldest existing religious document to contain references to such doctrines, but many years after His death, the Later Avestan Texts and Pahlavi literature gradually transformed His concise afterlife doctrines into a full-blown eschatology.

The Gathas
The Gathas provide a brief yet colorful account of the fate of the soul immediately after death. First, each soul undergoes an individual judgment at the Chinvat Bridge (Bridge of the Judge/Separator). Zoroaster Himself acts as the judge at this bridge. The record of each soul is read and the balance of good and evil deeds is cast. If good deeds predominate over evil, Zoroaster's 'pointing of the hand' will be toward heaven or paradise. If evil deeds outweigh good acts, Zoroaster's hand will point to the abyss (hell) below the bridge. Next, the judged souls must cross the Chinvat Bridge, which stretches over hell. The Gathas' description of this crossing is dramatic; righteous souls will be guided by Zoroaster Himself and will have no difficulty crossing the bridge and entering paradise of 'the House of Song,' where they will see their creator:

> Whichever man or woman, O Mazda Ahura, who would
> give to me the life of the Spirit which Thou knowest to be

the best, will receive the blessing of the Divine Law and the
Lord's Might and Majesty through the Good Mind. And
those whom I shall draw towards Your adoration, forth with
them all will I cross the Bridge Chinvat. (Yasna 46. 10)

The Gathas describe paradise as "the best existence," the abode of "the
best thought," where the sun never ceases to shine. There, the righteous
will experience eternal life, happiness, and the blessings of Ahura Mazda,
the creator.[5] Evil souls, however, find themselves unable to go beyond the
center of the bridge. Their own conscience (*daena*) will begin to torment
them and eventually will force them to plunge to their doom:

> Their own Soul and their own Self [*daena*] will torment them
> when they come to the Bridge of the Separator. To all time
> will they be guests for the House of the Lie. (Yasna 46. 11)

Thus, evil souls will dwell in "the House of the Lie" or hell forever. The
Gathas describe this place as the abode of "the worst thought," and say
that life in "the House of the Lie" is "the worst existence." In this place, evil
souls will forever suffer "alone."[6]

The Later Avestan Texts

The Later Avestan Texts provide further accounts of the first few days of
the life of the soul in the next world. One of them, Hadhokht Nask, notes
that before an individual judgment is passed on a soul, it remains near its
body for three days and nights. These days and nights are filled with happiness and confidence for righteous souls, and with anguish and fear for
wicked souls.

> At the end of the third night, when the dawn appears, the
> soul of the righteous man seems to be among plants, and to
> be inhaling fragrant odors. There seems to blow towards
> him, from the regions of the south, a wind fragrant, more
> fragrant than all others. (Hadhokht Nask 7)

Then, the *daena* (conscience) of the deceased appears to the soul in the

19

shape of a beautiful maiden, if righteous, or a hideous hag, if wicked. The maiden is "beautiful, radiant, white-armed, robust, fair-faced, erect, high breasted, of stately form, noble born, of glorious lineage, fifteen years old in appearance, as beautiful in form as the most beautiful of creatures" (Hadhokht Nask 9). She "appears amid a breath of balmy wind, fragrant with scents and perfumes."[7]

When the righteous soul asks the maiden who she is, she answers that she is the personification of his beautiful conscience, the fruit of his own good words, deeds, and thoughts. The soul of the righteous will then begin to rejoice and will enter a beautiful and fragrant region. Conversely, wicked souls go through a very unpleasant experience:

> At the end of the third night, O holy Zarathustra, when the dawn appears, the soul of the wicked man seems to be amid frosts and to be inhaling stenches. There seems to blow towards him, from the region of the north, a wind foul-smelling – more foul-smelling than all others. (Hadhokht Nask 25)

Then the conscience of the wicked soul appears to him in the form of an ugly hag. When the terrified soul asks the hag who she is, she responds that she is the personification of his own conscience, the fruit of his own evil words, deeds, and thoughts.

On the fourth day, the soul is taken to the seat of judgment – the Chinvat Bridge. If the soul is righteous, his guide will be the lovely maiden:

> She leads by hand the soul of the righteous, naturally exalted to the peak of the mountain, across the bridge of judgment, a spiritual admirable bridge. (Vendidad/Videvdat 19.30)

Wicked souls are dragged to the Chinvat Bridge by the demon Vizaresha. Interestingly, in the Later Avestan Texts, Zoroaster is no longer the judge at the Chinvat Bridge. Instead, a triad of heavenly judges – Mithra and his two assistants Sraosha and Rashnu – pass judgment. Mithra pre-dated

Zoroaster. He was the popular god of light and truth, and later of the sun, in ancient Persian mythology. The monotheist Zoroaster had condemned the worship of Mithra and other Persian mythological gods. However, over time, Mithra returned to favor among Persians.

The presence of Mithra and his two assistants changes the nature of judgment in Zoroaster's religion. The duties of passing judgment are now distributed among three personalities. Mithra oversees the judgment and Rashnu holds the dreaded scales to weigh the soul's merits and demerits; the role of Sraosha is not clear. After the weighing, Mithra issues the final verdict. Wicked souls are dragged to hell by Vizaresha, while the righteous are led across the Chinvat Bridge and conducted to heaven by the lovely maiden.[8]

Pahlavi Literature

The Pahlavi texts support most accounts in the Later Avestan Texts, and go on to describe further what happens to the soul during the first four days after death. The chief Pahlavi text, the Bundahishn – literally, 'the original creation' – states that on the first three nights after death, the demon Vizaresha along with his devilish crew tries to entrap the righteous soul by casting a noose (band) around its neck in order to drag it off to hell. But in spite of all their efforts, Vizaresha and his cohorts fail, the snare falls off and the righteous soul is released.[9] Then, in addition to the maiden, a fat cow and a garden appear before the righteous soul:

> Then there comes before it on the way the form of a cow,
> fat and full of milk, from which happiness and sweetness
> come to the soul.
>
> Secondly, there comes before it the form of a Maiden, a
> beautiful form in white raiment and fifteen years of age, who
> is fair from every side, and at whom the soul is pleased.
>
> Thirdly, there comes the form of a garden full of fresh
> fruits, full of water, full of dried fruits, and full of fertility,
> from which come joyous and happy thoughts to the soul.
> (Iranian Bundahishn 30, 4–5)

The wicked soul sees the opposite: a hideous hag, a lean cow, and a barren garden. The Bundahishn account of souls crossing the Chinvat

Bridge is also somewhat different from earlier Zoroastrian scriptures. Here, in the middle part of the bridge:

> There is a sharp edge which stands like a sword . . . and Hell is below the Bridge. Then the soul is carried to where stands the sharp edge. Then, if it be righteous, the sharp edge presents its broad side . . . If the soul be wicked, that sharp end continues to stand edgewise, and does not give a passage . . . With three steps which it [the soul] takes forward – which are the evil thoughts, evil words, and evil deeds that it has performed – it is cut down from the head of the Bridge, and falls headlong to Hell. (Ibid., I, 9–13)

Later Pahlavi texts claim that the personification of one's conscience – the maiden or the hag – appears to the soul halfway across the Chinvat Bridge:

> When it [the righteous soul] takes a step over the Chinvat Bridge, there comes to it a fragrant wind from Paradise, which smells of musk and ambergris, and that fragrance is more pleasant to it than any other pleasure. When it reaches the middle of the Bridge, it beholds an apparition of such beauty that it hath never seen a figure of greater beauty. . .
>
> And when the apparition appears to the soul, it [the soul] speaks thus: "Who art thou with such beauty that a figure of greater beauty I have never seen?" The apparition speaks [thus]: "I am thine own good actions. I myself was good, but thine actions have made me better." And she embraces him, and they both depart with complete joy and ease to Paradise. (Sad Dar Bundahish 99, 5–9)

If the soul is judged as wicked, the case is very different:

> When it [the wicked soul] takes a step over the Chinvat Bridge, there blows . . . an exceedingly foul wind from Hell, so foul as is unheard of among all the stench in the world.

There is no stench fouler than that; and that stench is the worst of all the punishments that are visited upon it.

When it reaches the middle of the Chinvat Bridge, it sees an apparition of such extreme ugliness and frightfulness that it hath never seen one uglier and more unseemly. . . And it is as much terrified on account of her as a sheep is of a wolf, and wants to flee away from her. And that apparition speaks thus: "Whither dost thou want to flee?" It [the soul] speaks thus: "Who art thou with such ugliness and terror that a figure worse than thou art, uglier and more frightful, I have never seen in the world?"

She speaks [thus]: "I am thine own bad actions. I myself was ugly, and thou madest me worse day after day, and now thou hast thrown me and thine own self into misery and damnation, and we shall suffer punishment till the day of the Resurrection." And she embraces it, and both fall head-long from the middle of the Chinvat Bridge and descend to Hell. (Sad Dar Bundahish 99. 15–20)

Pahlavi texts also provide further accounts of the joys of heaven and the torments of hell, most of which are very tangible in form. For example, the Datastan-i-Denik's portrayal of heaven is of a lofty, pure, exalted place where all manner of physical comfort, pleasure and joy are found. Inhabitants of heaven are free from all hurt, pain, and discomfort. Various trees with luscious fruits, fields of corn, and all sorts of flowers and plants abound. The newly arrived soul is greeted by his friends, who tell him of all the delights awaiting him. This last account recalls what many individuals with out-of-body experiences have related.

The same text appears to corroborate something else that is frequently mentioned by those who have had near-death experiences – the instantaneous review of one's life. However, unlike out-of-body experiences where individuals have *panoramic* reviews of their lives, in this Zoroastrian book only the wicked souls are said to go through life-reviews, and these are very frightening because they only contain sins and crimes.

The greatest joy promised to the righteous is the vision of God, not in human form but in the form of pure light. There are striking parallels between this being of light and that described by those with near-death experiences. In both cases, the person who confronts the being of light is at first totally astonished by this encounter, and then the being begins to communicate telepathically. One Pahlavi book depicts this being of light (the Beauteous Vision) as follows: "And when Ahuramazd [God] spoke in this manner, I remained astonished, for I saw a light, but I saw nobody; I also heard a voice, and I understood that: 'This is Ahuramazd.'"[10]

The Pahlavi texts go to great lengths to paint a detailed picture of hell and the various torments that await the wicked there. The Datastan-i-Denik says hell is "sunken, deep, and ascending, most dark, most stinking, and most terrible, most supplied with wretched existences . . . in it there is no comfort, pleasantness or joy."[11] The wickeds' only companions in hell are the demons who are there to torment them. But hell is not a permanent state; it only lasts until the final rehabilitation at the end of time.

GENERAL ESCHATOLOGY

First intimations of a general eschatology in Zoroastrianism are found in the Gathas. In Later Avestan and Pahlavi texts, these ideas gradually evolve into coherent doctrines. One such doctrine teaches that, at the end of time, in a last great struggle between God (Ahuramazd) and the power of evil (Ahriman), the latter is totally annihilated. This final victory of good over evil is then followed by the general resurrection of humanity.

Next, the resurrected must pass through molten metal to be purged of sin. For the righteous, this seemingly excruciating process will be as painless as bathing in warm milk. For the wicked, however, it will be extremely painful. Fortunately for them, this agonizing experience lasts only three days. Following this universal purification, the whole human race will begin to enjoy happiness, and will peacefully coexist like members of one large family.[12]

Eventually, Zoroastrian eschatology came to leave its mark on both Jewish and Islamic eschatologies. Even a cursory look at these religions reveals significant parallels in their afterlife doctrines, and some of these similarities are so striking that many scholars believe the later Jewish and

Islamic eschatologies borrowed doctrines in whole or in part from Zoroastrian literature. Jewish adoptions of Zoroastrian beliefs probably happened during the Persian rule over Babylon, while Islamic appropriations are likely to have taken place following the Muslim conquest of Persia after 651 CE.

A clear example of such borrowings by the Jews is the concept of bodily resurrection, which first appeared in Zoroaster's Gathas. Centuries after Zoroaster, the Jewish prophet Ezekiel's oracles of hope, which he delivered between 585 and 568 BCE, make reference to this doctrine. Ezekiel evidently had a vision of a vast plain covered with dry human bones, bleached by the sun, which is much like the Zoroastrian funeral ground. Ancient Zoroastrians never buried their dead, but left bodies outside under the sun in *dakhmahs* (see Illustration 2), which are open structures built on remote, barren hilltops. This allowed vultures to strip the flesh from the bones of the dead without contaminating the soil. They were convinced that God would reassemble the scattered parts of bodies during the general resurrection.

After Ezekiel sees the plain with human bones, he is commanded by God to prophesy to the bones and announce their resurrection (Ezekiel 37: 1–13). The skeletons are then immediately reassembled to form bodies (see Illustration 7). Finally, God asks the prophet to make the winds breathe life into the bodies. (This prophecy symbolizes the ability of the newly resurrected Jewish people to leave their life of captivity and exile in Babylon for eternal freedom in their homeland of Palestine.[13]) The Qur'án, the Muslims' holy book, also reaffirms the Zoroastrian belief in physical resurrection.

Zoroastrian eschatology is among the richest and most original of all living eschatologies. The afterlife doctrines of Zoroastrianism introduced a number of novel ideas that were later appropriated by Jewish, Christian, and Muslim sources, either wholly or partially. Among these are the concept of a struggle between the forces of good and evil, which in later western religions turns into the battle between God and Satan; the belief that humanity has an immortal soul that conquers death; belief in individual judgment after death, and in a universal physical resurrection for all humanity in the fullness of time; and features such as the balance for weighing human deeds and a bridge that stretches over hell and reaches into heaven.

NOTES

1. J. R. Hinnells (ed.), *The Facts on File Dictionary of Religions*, p. 361

2. Ibid., p. 362

3. Ibid.

4. Ibid., p. 57

5. R. C. Zaehner, *The Dawn and Twilight of Zoroastrianism*, p. 57

6. D. S. Noss and J. B. Noss, *A History of the World's Religions*, p. 364

7. J. D. C. Pavry, *The Zoroastrian Doctrine of a Future Life: From Death to the Individual Judgment*, p. 33

8. Ibid., p. 66

9. Ibid., p. 15

10. M. Haug and E. W. West, *The Book of Arda Viraf*, p. 203

11. E. W. West, *The Sacred Books of the East: Pahlavi Texts*, vol. 8, p. 58

12. C. J. Bleeker and G. Widengren, *Historia Religionum*, vol. 1, p. 368

13. C. McDannell and B. Lang, *Heaven: A History*, pp. 12–13

GLOSSARY

Ahura Mazda: 'The Wise Lord.' Supreme deity (God) in Zoroastrianism.

Avesta: 'The Scriptures' or 'Wisdom/Knowledge.' The most sacred book of Zoroastrianism, it contains writings that both pre- and post-date Zoroaster. Only seventeen hymns, known as the Gathas or Hymns of Zoroaster, can be attributed to Zoroaster with reasonable certainty.

Avestan: An East Iranian language of the Indo-European family with close ties to Vedic, the language of the Hindu Vedas; Avestan is the language of all the Avesta, except the Gathas.

Bundahishn: 'The Original Creation.' The chief Pahlavi text which, among other things, provides detailed accounts of the fate of the soul on the first three nights after death.

Chinvat Bridge: 'Bridge of the Judge' or 'Separator' where good souls are separated from evil ones during individual judgment.

Daena: 'Self' or 'Conscience.' The higher religious self of a human being; the moral center or personality.

Dakhmah: 'Tower of Silence,' where many Indian Zoroastrians (Parsis) dispose of their dead.

Datastan-i-Denik: A well-known Pahlavi text.

Gathas: The seventeen 'Hymns' or 'Songs' of Zoroaster. The only part of the Avesta whose authorship can, with any degree of certainty, be attributed to Zoroaster.

Hadhokht Nask: A Later Avestan Text.

House of the Lie: Hell.

House of Song: Paradise or heaven.

Later Avestan Texts: Certain Zoroastrian texts written in the Avestan language many years after Zoroaster revealed the Gathas.

Mithra: The popular god of light and truth, and later of the sun in ancient Persian mythology; appears as a sub-deity or angel in Later Avestan mythology; replaces Zoroaster as the main judge at the Chinvat Bridge in the Later Avestan Texts.

Pahlavi: Middle Persian, the official language of Persia during the Sassanian dynasty (226–651CE).

Pahlavi Texts: Zoroastrian sacred literature of the third to the tenth centuries written in the Pahlavi language; includes most extant Zoroastrian texts.

Rashnu: One of the two assistants of Mithra, the judge of the dead. Rashnu is the one who holds the scales for weighing the soul's good and evil deeds.

Sad Dar Bundahish: A Pahlavi text.

Sraosha: One of the two assistants of Mithra, the judge of the dead.

Vizaresha: A demon, in Later Avestan and Pahlavi literature, who drags the wicked to hell.

Zand: Translations of and commentaries on the Avesta. The only surviving Zand is in the Pahlavi language.

CHAPTER 3
JUDAISM

INTRODUCTION

The monotheistic religion preached by Moses had its roots in Semitic paganism; at Sinai, Moses began to shape Jewish pagan beliefs into the worship of Yahweh (God) alone, and introduced a corresponding body of social and ritual laws that met the needs of the Jews in their desert surroundings.

The evolution of Judaism over the centuries has brought many transformations in the social, political, religious, and cultural lives of the Jewish people. For example, in the agricultural period of Canaan (biblical Palestine), Judaism acquired a sophisticated sacrificial cult, ceremonies and festivals, an organized priesthood, and codes of law. The institution of kingship was established and prophets appeared who advanced the cause of ethical monotheism and criticized the ritualistic practices of the masses.

Later, the Babylonian exile signaled the breakup of the geographical unity of the Jews and the scattering of their population to various parts of the ancient world. Sovereignty over the Jews fell to the Persians, Greeks, and Romans. Over time, states *An Encyclopedia of Religion*, the messianic hopes and eschatological yearnings of the politically crushed Jews merged with the mystery cults of neighboring peoples and, "centering in the person of Jesus, formed the world religion of Christianity."[1] In modern times, Jewish hopes of national and political unity spawned the Zionist movement, which succeeded in restoring Jewish sovereignty over parts of ancient Palestine and resulted in the settling of many Jews in their historical homeland. The religion preached by Moses has, over the centuries, produced many schools of thought, including the Hellenistic, Talmudic, Orthodox, Neo-Orthodox, Conservative, and Reform movements. Here, however, we concentrate on the early biblical and post-biblical material.

SACRED LITERATURE

The Tanach (The Hebrew Bible, also known as the Old Testament)
Judaism divides the Tanach into the following:

Torah (The Law)
Broadly, the Torah signifies the total content of God's unceasing revelation to Israel. In a narrower sense, it refers to the first five books of the Hebrew Bible (the Pentateuch) which are also known as the Five Books of Moses. Orthodox Jews believe these books contain all the laws revealed by God to Moses.

Prophets
These canonical books include the writings of well-known Jewish prophets such as Isaiah, Jeremiah, Ezekiel, Zechariah, and others.

The Writings (Hagiography/Sacred Writings)
These include such works as the Song of Solomon, Psalms, Proverbs, Job, Daniel, and Ezra.

Apocalyptic Literature
These writings flourished in the late Jewish and early Christian eras (165 BCE–120 CE). The authorship of most apocalyptic works is in question. Most of these writings encouraged the Jewish faithful to remain steadfast in the face of cruelties they were enduring in captivity. The main purpose of these books was to give Jews hope and confidence that the evil age would soon come to a dramatic close. "The world would literally come to en end. Fire would consume the world and purify it from evil. The righteous would then rise and take their place in a new and purified world."[2]

Some Jews believe the authors of the apocalyptic works were great figures of the past such as Adam, Noah, Abraham, Moses, and Ezra. Orthodox Jews, however, have consistently refused to recognize the authenticity of these writings. Parts of the Assumptions of Moses, I Enoch and II Enoch, as well as IV Ezra are among well-known Jewish apocalyptic literature.

Pseudepigraphic (Apocryphal) Literature

As with many apocalyptic writings, the origin and authorship of pseudepigraphic works are in doubt. These include writings that have scriptural form or content but are not included in official Jewish scripture, and are considered by many Jews as 'outside books' or 'heretical books.' The afterlife doctrines of this class of Jewish writings are considered here because early Judaism has little to say about death or life after death. Among the important pseudepigraphic writings are Psalms of Solomon, Tobit, Ecclesiasticus, I Enoch and the Assumptions of Moses, 7–30.

The Talmud (Instruction)

The Talmud is a collection of Jewish traditions supplementing the Hebrew Bible. It is known as the Oral Torah because, for centuries, it was explained and transmitted orally to following generations by Jewish rabbis. Though the main focus of the Talmud is Jewish law, it also contains lengthy discussions on history, ethics, religion, science, folklore, and social institutions. The two layers of the Talmud are Mishnah (Repeat or Study) and the commentaries known as Gemara (Learning). In many ways this is the most important material for Jews, but in this chapter we concentrate on the foundation documents of Judaism.

PERSONAL ESCHATOLOGY

Close examination of the Hebrew Bible reveals no systematic personal eschatology. Although one can find references to 'paradise,' 'heaven,' and 'hell,' these terms do not carry any consistent meaning in the Hebrew Bible. There is also no mention of an immortal soul that conquers death, nor any clear indication of exactly what remains of the individual at death.

But some entity is left, and it "goes down" to a dark and gloomy place called Sheol (the pit). Sheol is a subterranean hollow in the lowest depths of the earth, and it is the eternal abode of all the dead, righteous and unrighteous alike (Psalms 63: 9, 86: 13; Ezekiel 26: 20, 31: 14). The dark, heavy and impassive character of Sheol makes the general picture of afterlife in the Hebrew Bible atypically melancholic and judgment-free: "I go where I shall not return, even to the land of darkness and death, without any order, and where the light is as darkness" (Job 10: 21–22).

At times, the Hebrew Bible portrays Sheol as a prison with bars:

Bring me out of prison that I may give thanks to thy name.
(Psalms 142: 7)
Will it go down to the bars of Sheol?
Shall we descend together into the dust? (Job 17: 16)

Job 30: 23 identifies Sheol as the eternal abode of all the dead, righteous or unrighteous: "I know that Thou wilt bring me to death to the dwelling appointed for every living man." Sheol is also signified as the land of forgetfulness (Psalms 88: 12), of silence (Psalms 94: 17), of destruction (Job 26: 6, 28: 22), and of dust (Daniel 12: 2; Job 7: 21, 17: 16).

There is no praise of God in Sheol: "The dead do not praise the Lord, nor do any that go down into silence" (Psalms 115: 17). The dead are devoid of their material possessions: "He will not be rich, nor his wealth endure, nor his possessions reach the Nether world" (Job 15: 29). They have no knowledge of the events that take place on earth: "His [the dead's] sons achieve honor, but he never knows. They are disgraced, but he perceives not" (Job 14: 21). Existence in Sheol is marked by inactivity and stagnation: "There is no work or account or knowledge or wisdom in Sheol" (Ecclesiastes 9: 10).

Once entered into Sheol, there is no return to the land of the living: "As the cloud fades and vanishes, so he who goes down to Sheol does not come up" (Job 7: 9). The inhabitants of Sheol are in a state of permanent sleep: "Man lies down and never rises. They rouse not from their sleep" (Job 14: 12).

Heaven and Hell

As noted above, the terms heaven and hell do not carry their generally accepted meanings in the Hebrew Bible. Heaven is identified as the dwelling-place of God (Kings 8: 30) where He sits on His throne (Isaiah 66: 1). Hell or Gehenna is mentioned as a valley (the valley of the son of Hinnom) south of Jerusalem where the pre-Israelite Canaanites sacrificed their children to the god Moloch (Joshua 15: 8, 18: 16; II Kings 23: 10; Jeremiah 7: 31, 32: 35; II Chronicles 28: 3, 33: 6). This valley was also used to bury criminals and to burn Jerusalem's garbage. However, later Jewish

LIFE AFTER DEATH: A STUDY OF THE AFTERLIFE IN WORLD RELIGIONS

works borrowed the negative connotations of the valley of Gehenna and conceptualized hell as the eternal abode of wicked souls.[3]

Therefore, the notion of heaven and hell as diametrically opposed places where individuals go to receive reward or retribution for their deeds is non-existent in the Old Testament. The deathly, judgment-free concept of Sheol leaves no room for individual judgment of souls. A paradisal place called Gan Eden (the Garden of Eden) is mentioned, but this should not be equated with heaven as the only inhabitants of Gan Eden were the first man and woman – Adam and Eve – before their fall. Some sources place the location of this garden in the Euphrates valley in today's Iraq.

There are many artistic renditions of the Garden of Eden. German painter Lucas Cranach's work is one of the most well known (see Illustration 4). Cranach's sixteenth-century painting illustrates six different events recorded in the book of Genesis. In the background, God creates the first man, Adam, then the first woman, Eve, from Adam's rib. Satan deceives Eve, the couple are shamed by God and expelled from the garden. In the foreground, God is seen warning Adam and Eve about Satan's intrigues before the couple's fall.

Second Century BCE Apocalyptic and Pseudepigraphic Literature

Ecclesiasticus
This work upholds most Old Testament views about our fate after death. Everyone, good or evil, is sent to Sheol and plunged into a permanent sleep (46: 19). There is no praise of God in Sheol: "Thanksgiving perishes from the dead as from one that is not" (17: 28). There is also no retribution beyond the grave, and no account is taken of one's life on earth: "Fear not death, whether it be ten or a hundred or a thousand years, there are no chastisements for life in Sheol" (41: 3–4).

But Ecclesiasticus is also among the first Jewish writings to formulate a personal system of retribution for the wicked. While it maintains the Old Testament's judgment-free view of Sheol, it does suggest punishment for the wicked while still on earth: "The ungodly . . . shall not go unpunished unto Hades" (9: 12). If the wicked person does not pay for his evil deeds, his children will: "The inheritance of sinners' children shall perish. And with their posterity abideth poverty" (41: 6).

Tobit

This work also maintains the traditional view of Sheol as a place where existence comes to a halt (3: 10, 13: 2), and where the departed abide forever: "Command my spirit to be taken from me, that I may become earth . . . and go to the everlasting place" (3: 6).

I Enoch and II Enoch

These books supposedly recount the divinely guided journeys of the Jewish patriarch Enoch through the earth and the seven heavens. During these journeys Enoch is said to have discovered all the mysteries of heaven and earth. In his two books, he shares these mysteries with humankind. However, I Enoch, which was written between the third and first centuries BCE, contains several books by different unknown authors. II Enoch was probably written in Egypt during the first century CE, and its authorship is also in question.

I Enoch 6–36 is the first Jewish literary work to relinquish the traditional views of Sheol as a judgment-free abode of all in favor of an explicitly moral Sheol where righteous and wicked souls await a final judgment. For the first time, Sheol is divided into compartments for various souls. There are three compartments, with the first assigned to righteous souls, the second to sinners who died without receiving punishment on earth, and the third to sinners who did receive retribution while still on earth.

Of these three groups, the first two will remain in their compartments until the Day of Judgment, when they are resurrected for the final judgment. While there, the sinners who died without receiving due punishment are given a foretaste of the horrible fate that awaits them in Gehenna (hell) following the final judgment. Occupants of the third compartment (sinners who received their due punishment on earth) will receive no further judgment, and Sheol becomes their final abode.

First Century BCE Apocalyptic and Pseudepigraphic Literature

I Enoch 37–70 (Similitudes)

A major contribution of the Similitudes to Jewish personal eschatology is the idea of a new temporary dwelling place for righteous souls before their resurrection. This place is paradise. Upon death, the souls of the righteous will go there while those of the wicked go to Sheol. Every soul awaits resurrection in one of these two temporary abodes, paradise or Sheol.

I Enoch 91-104
This is the first Jewish work to equate Sheol with Gehenna. Thus, upon death, only the souls of the wicked are sent to Sheol, which is very dark and full of flames. There, the wicked souls are bound in chains, to suffer continuous punishment. By contrast, the souls of the righteous remain in a state of respite and are guarded by angels until the general resurrection.

First Century CE Apocalyptic and Pseudepigraphic Literature

II Enoch
This work envisions both human souls and fallen angels living in intermediate places till the Day of Judgment. Interestingly, it claims that even the souls of animals are preserved until the last judgment, so they can testify against people who ill-treated them (58: 5–6).

GENERAL ESCHATOLOGY

Numerous passages in various books of the Hebrew Bible point to a general eschatology for humankind. Some are vague, others are more specific. Daniel (12: 1–13) and Isaiah (26: 1–19) anticipate a general resurrection for humanity during which God will issue a final, binding judgment on every individual. Daniel 12: 2 states: "Many of them that sleep in the dust shall awake, some to everlasting life, and some to reproaches and everlasting abhorrence." Jeremiah (23: 5–6) explains that, following this general resurrection and final judgment, God will send a descendant of King David to establish His kingdom on earth. This holy figure will bring justice and righteousness to the land and the faithful will live in peace and tranquility:

> Behold, the days are coming, says the Lord, when I will raise
> up for David a righteous Branch, and he shall reign as king
> and deal wisely and shall execute justice and righteousness
> in the land. In his days Judah will be saved, and Israel will

dwell securely. And this is the name by which he will be
called: the Lord is our righteousness.

In this kingdom, men will be revived by the spirit of God (Joel 2: 28–32;
Jeremiah 31: 33; Ezekiel 36: 25–28). All nations will come to worship at
Jerusalem (Isaiah 2: 2–4). The site of this kingdom will be a renewed and
glorified Holy Land.[4]

Second Century BCE Apocalyptic and Pseudepigraphic Literature

Ecclesiasticus
Ecclesiasticus reaffirms the Old Testament's anticipation of the establishment of a messianic kingdom (36: 1–17) on earth. Elijah will be the
forerunner of this event (48: 10). With the establishment of this eternal
kingdom, Israel is released from evil (50: 23–24) and the scattered tribes
are restored (36: 11).

Tobit
Like the Old Testament, Tobit expresses high hopes for the future of
Israel. Thus, following a universal resurrection, Jerusalem will be rebuilt
and its temple will be reconstructed with gold and precious stones. The
scattered tribes will be restored, and the heathen nations will abandon
their own gods and worship the God of Israel.[5]

I Enoch 6–36
As noted above, in this work Sheol is for the first time divided into three
compartments, one for righteous souls, one for sinners who were not pun-
ished on earth, and one for sinners who did receive due punishment in
their lifetime.

When the Day of Judgment arrives, the inhabitants of the first two
compartments of Sheol – the righteous and the sinners who escaped punishment on earth – are resurrected. The latter do not experience a true resurrection, but instead the life of stagnation in Sheol is replaced by a life
of everlasting punishment in Gehenna. The righteous souls, on the other
hand, experience a genuine resurrection of the body, eat of the tree of life
(25: 4–6), and enjoy patriarchal lives (25: 6) in an eternal messianic king-

dom on a purified earth (10: 7, 16, 20–22) with Jerusalem as its center (25: 5).[6]

First Century BCE Apocalyptic and Pseudepigraphic Literature

I Enoch 37–70 (Similitudes)
The Similitudes revert to earlier Jewish concepts of a general resurrection and a final judgment for all humankind, followed by the establishment of a messianic kingdom on earth. This kingdom will be established by a superhuman Messiah. The Similitudes are the first Jewish writings to mention the four titles for the Messiah, which afterwards occur frequently in the New Testament. These titles are 'The Anointed One [Christ]' (48: 10, 52: 4); 'The Righteous One' (38: 2, 53: 6; Acts 3: 14, 5: 52, 22: 14); 'The Elect One' (40: 5, 45: 3–4; Luke 9: 35, 23: 35); and 'The Son of Man'.

The Messiah is considered to be the judge of both men and angels. On the Day of Judgment, He will judge all men and angels according to their deeds, which are weighed in balances (49: 1). Following this binding judgment, wicked men and fallen angels are destroyed and the present heaven and earth are transformed into a new heaven and earth where the Messiah establishes His eternal kingdom. Then, the righteous are resurrected in angelic bodies and dwell in this eternal messianic kingdom to enjoy the company of the Messiah and grow in knowledge and righteousness.

I Enoch 91-104
This work introduces a number of new concepts that significantly change the face of Jewish general eschatology. Older Jewish writings envisioned a general resurrection and a final judgment for all humankind, following which an eternal messianic kingdom was to be established on earth. However, this book anticipates a temporary earthly kingdom before the general resurrection and final judgment. In addition, on the Day of Judgment the earth is destroyed and replaced by a new heaven. The righteous are then resurrected in spirit and they enter this new heaven to become companions of the heavenly hosts (104: 6). Like stars, they will shine forever.

Psalms of Solomon
Psalms 1–16 make reference to a temporary messianic kingdom. There is

no mention of a Messiah. When the appointed time arrives, the kingdom expires, and is followed by spiritual resurrection for the righteous, who will continue to enjoy eternal life and happiness. The wicked, however, descend into Sheol or Gehenna immediately after death and will be tortured there for eternity.

Psalms 17–19 also envision a temporary messianic kingdom, but they also give accounts of the Messiah who is to establish and rule over this kingdom. Specific details of the Messiah's ancestry as well as His victories are provided. It is prophesied that the Messiah will be of David's lineage and will be called the Christ (17: 36, 18: 6, 8). He will be a righteous king (17: 35) who will purge Jerusalem, restore its sanctity (17: 33), and will make Israel a holy people (17: 29, 30, 36). He will also destroy the ungodly nations by the word of His mouth. Eventually, this Messiah will either destroy or subdue all the hostile nations.

First Century CE Apocalyptic and Pseudepigraphic Literature

Assumptions of Moses

All that is left of this work today is a fragment of a larger piece of apocalyptic writing now lost. It contains views on Jewish general eschatology, and one of its prophecies states that 1,750 years after the death of Moses, God will intervene on behalf of Israel and the ten tribes of Israel will be restored. Next, a temporary messianic kingdom will be established on earth. In due time this will expire and Israel will be exalted to heaven. From heaven, it shall see its enemies in Gehenna (10: 7–10):

> For the Most High will arise, the Eternal God alone,
> And he will appear to punish the Gentiles,
> And he will destroy all their idols.
> Then thou, O Israel, wilt be happy,
> And thou wilt mount upon the neck of the eagle,
> And the days of thy mourning will be ended.
> And God will exalt thee,
> And he will cause thee to approach to the heaven of stars,
> And he will establish thy habitation among them.
> And thou wilt look from on high and wilt see thy enemies in Gehenna,

And thou wilt recognize them and rejoice,
And thou wilt give thanks and confess thy Creator.

II Enoch

The general eschatology of II Enoch presents several notions that had significant impact on later Christian and Islamic eschatologies. For instance, it is prophesied that, after 6,000 years of world history, humankind will experience a thousand years of rest and blessedness, as the six days of creation were followed by one day of rest. This period is the same as the time of the messianic kingdom spoken of in older Jewish sacred literature. Here, for the first time, a specific duration of 1,000 years has been allotted to this kingdom. At its close, all people are to be judged during "the Day of Judgment" (39: 1), "the great day of the Lord" (18: 6), "the great judgment" (58: 5, 65: 6), or "the eternal judgment" (7: 1). Then, the righteous will be sent to their final abode in the third heaven.

In the midst of paradise is the tree of life. It is on this tree that God rests when He visits the paradise. The excellence and sweet odor of this tree are beyond description. It is made of gold and crimson, but is transparent as fire. From the roots of this tree, four streams go forth which pour honey, milk, oil, and wine in four different directions. Three hundred glorious angels are the keepers of paradise, and they serve God with never-ceasing voices and blessed singing.

Naturally, the fate of the wicked souls is very different. They are cast into hell, also located in the third heaven, and are tormented there forever. This hell is a gloomy place filled with all manner of torture. Its guardians resemble terrifying serpents. The faces of these guardians are like extinguished lamps, while their eyes are like darkened flames.

IV Ezra (The Fourth Ezra)

This is an important apocalyptic work. Though Ezra, the well-known biblical hero, is considered by some the sole author of this book, many think it to be of composite authorship. The Fourth Ezra deals mainly with general eschatology. This work anticipates a temporary messianic kingdom in which the Messiah will rule over the world for 400 years. At the close of this period, the Messiah and all other living creatures will die, and the earth will be dead for seven days. This is followed by the resurrection of humankind during which the dead of all generations, righteous and unrighteous, will rise from their tombs and appear before the throne of God in a final judgment. Then the righteous and wicked are sent to their eternal abodes – paradise and Gehenna.

Perhaps the course of Jewish eschatology through the centuries can best be characterized as a story that began in total despair and gradually changed to hope not only for survival but for everlasting glory. The early beliefs of Judaism about the afterlife are markedly different from those of the other western religions considered in this book (Zoroastrianism, Christianity, Islam, and the Bahá'í Faith). Early Jewish beliefs are characterized by hopelessness and disillusionment, which could be a consequence of the repeated Jewish enslavement by others. The afterlife doctrines of the most authoritative Jewish work, the Hebrew Bible, form a clear example of this. There is no mention of a personal judgment at death; rather, an entity which is all that remains of us descends to a gloomy place called Sheol, where it sleeps until general resurrection. While there are references to a garden (the Garden of Eden) and Gehenna (hell) in the Hebrew Bible, there is no mention of the traditional heaven and hell as the abodes of righteous and wicked souls. Many years later, Zoroastrian influences led the authors of other Jewish works gradually to change the nature of Sheol from a judgment-free state to a place of retribution for various souls. Later Jewish books also began to incorporate the traditional heaven and hell as places of recompense for our earthly deeds. With these changes, the earlier disillusionment of Jewish texts began to give way to hope for a savior (Messiah) who would come to the rescue of Jewish people, rid the earth of their enemies, and establish a temporary kingdom on earth. This kingdom would be followed by a general resurrection and a final judgment for all.

NOTES

1. V. Ferm (ed.), *An Encyclopedia of Religion*, p. 403

2. Ibid., p. 30

3. R. J. Werblowsky and G. Wigoder, *The Encyclopedia of Jewish Religion*, p. 153

4. C. Pilcher and D. D. Oxon, *The Hereafter in Jewish and Christian Thought*, p. 51

5. R. H. Charles, *Eschatology: The Doctrine of a Future Life in Israel: Judaism and Christianity*, p. 170

6. Ibid., pp. 215–19

GLOSSARY

Apocalyptic Literature: A class of non-canonical literature which flourished in the late Jewish and early Christian era. Its purpose was to give hope of a better future to the Hebrews in captivity. Parts of II Enoch (Secrets of Enoch) and the Assumptions of Moses are examples of Jewish apocalyptic writings.

Apocryphal Literature: See "Pseudepigraphic Literature."

Ecclesiasticus: This book was written about 180 BCE. The author of Ecclesiasticus is generally considered to be Jesus, the son of Sirach, and this book is sometimes known by the name of its author. In content and spirit, Ecclesiasticus is similar to the biblical Ecclesiastes and Proverbs.

I Enoch and II Enoch: Apocalyptic works of composite authorship, attributed to the Jewish patriarch Enoch. They describe the divinely guided journeys of Enoch through the earth and heavens and the discoveries he makes.

Gehenna: 'Hell.' In the Old Testament, a valley south of Jerusalem where the pre-Israelite Canaanites sacrificed their children to the god Moloch. This valley was also used to bury criminals and burn Jerusalem's garbage. Post-biblical literature borrowed the negative connotations of this valley and conceptualized a hell that is the eternal abode of wicked souls.

Hagiographa: 'Sacred Writings.' See "Writings."

Hebrew Bible: See "Tanach."

Messiah: 'Anointed.' The promised and expected deliverer of the Jewish people; broadly applied to kings and holy figures in various Jewish writings.

Old Testament: See "Tanach."

Pentateuch: The first five books of the Old Testament.

Prophets: The second of three Jewish divisions of the Old Testament which includes the writings of various Jewish prophets such as Isaiah, Jeremiah, and Ezekiel.

Psalms of Solomon: A pseudepigraphic work written about the middle of the first century BCE. Jewish tradition has mistakenly ascribed authorship of this book to Solomon. The book contains eighteen psalms patterned after the biblical psalms.

Pseudepigraphic Literature: Like apocalyptic literature, many pseudepigraphic writings are of questionable origin and authorship. These writings have scriptural form or content but are non-canonical. The Psalms of Solomon, Tobit, and Ecclesiasticus are well-known examples of pseudepigraphic works.

Sheol: 'Pit.' A subterranean hollow in the lowest depths of the earth, originally the eternal abode of all the dead, righteous and unrighteous alike.

Talmud: 'Instruction.' A collection of Jewish traditions which supplement the Old Testament. It is known as the Oral Torah. The primary authors of the Talmud were Jewish rabbis.

Tanach: The Hebrew Bible containing the Torah (Pentateuch), the Prophets or Nebiim, and the Writings (Hagiographa) or Ketubim. Tanach is a vocalization of the Hebrew letters TNK. Christians include the Hebrew Bible in their Bible and call it the Old Testament.

Tobit: A pseudepigraphic writing composed about 200 BCE. Tobit was a devout Jew whose story is recorded in this book.

Torah: 'Law.' In broad terms, all Jewish revelation; in a narrower sense, the Pentateuch, the first of three Jewish divisions of the Old Testament.

Writings: The last of three Jewish divisions of the Old Testament. It includes such works as the Song of Solomon, Psalms, Proverbs, Job, Daniel, and Ezra.

CHAPTER 4
BUDDHISM

INTRODUCTION

L ike Hinduism, the term Buddhism refers to a diverse array of beliefs and practices and implies a degree of uniformity that does not exist, note David and John Noss in *A History of the World's Religions*.[1] After originating in India, Buddhism soon spread to various parts of Asia and eventually reached the western hemisphere in the nineteenth century. Today, different schools of Buddhist thought may be divided into four broad categories:

The Buddhism of South East Asia (the Theravada or 'Way of the Elders' school)
This is mainly practiced in Sri Lanka, Burma, Cambodia, Thailand, Laos, and Indonesia.

East Asian Buddhism (the Mahayana or 'Great Vehicle' school)
This is followed chiefly in China, Vietnam, Korea, and Japan.

Tibetan Buddhism (the Tantric or 'Indestructible Vehicle' school)
This occurs mainly in Tibet, Nepal, Bhutan, and Sikhim. In both theory and practice, this is essentially a development within the Mahayana school of Buddhism.

Western Buddhism
This is the kind practiced in Europe and North America.

SACRED LITERATURE

Shortly before His death, Buddha reportedly told His followers that, in His absence, the *Dharma* (His doctrines or teachings) would be their leader. Although early Buddhist thinkers took great pains to use Buddha's own words as the primary source for formulating and transmitting Buddhist doctrines, teachings, and rules for community living, no unadulterated collection of Buddha's sayings exists today. The different versions of the accepted scripture of Buddhism are sectarian variants of a body of work that took form during 300 years of oral transmission.[2]

As with Hinduism, the sacred literature of Buddhism is very diverse and complex. Most Buddhist scholars divide the wide array of scriptures into the Pali, Chinese, and Tibetan canons. Together, these include literally hundreds of volumes of work, containing thousands of texts which deal with a multitude of subjects.

The Pali Canon

This includes the Tripitaka (Three Baskets), which are early Buddhist scriptures in the Pali language comprised of three parts: Vinaya (Monastic Rules), Sutta (Discourses), and Abhidhamma (Supplementary Doctrines).

The Chinese Canon

This category includes numerous volumes on such diverse topics as the lives of various Buddhas, fables and parables, and manuals of rituals and spells. There are also scholastic treatises and commentaries on different sermons of Buddha, Buddhist encyclopedias and dictionaries, and works on Buddhist history and the biographies of significant Buddhist figures.

The Tibetan Canon

Included here are the Tibetan Tripitaka (Three Baskets) and many other texts that deal with the words and actions of Buddha and other tales. They also contain hymns of praise, commentaries on the sermons of Buddha, and technical treatises on logic, grammar, lexicography, poetics, medicine, and chemistry.

Buddhists, like Hindus, use the term *Dharma* or *Dhamma* (literally, 'the norm,' or 'that which is true') to refer to their belief system. The major difference in this regard between Hinduism and Buddhism is that

Hindu teachings come from many different sources, while Buddhist teachings and moral injunctions come from one man – Gautama Buddha (literally 'Enlightened One').

PERSONAL ESCHATOLOGY

As in Hinduism, the various schools of Buddhist thought offer different accounts of what happens to a person shortly before, during, and after the death of the physical body. These are too numerous and diverse to cover comprehensively in an introductory book, so we will focus only on the eschatological views adhered to by most Buddhists.

Like Hinduism, Buddhism is only concerned with *personal* eschatology; there is no mention of a collective destiny for humankind. Initially a reform movement within Hinduism, Buddhism maintains beliefs in the twin doctrines of transmigration and *karma*, which means that Buddhist notions of death and the afterlife are similar to those of Hinduism and therefore markedly different from the other major religions.

According to these beliefs, each person is reborn countless times and lives through different types of existences. The quality of his or her current life is a reflection of present and past *karma*. Hence, if the individual now lives a comfortable life, this is the reward of good deeds performed in present and past lives. In contrast, those experiencing misery can only blame themselves for evil deeds they are committing or have committed in previous existences. Thus the individual is held totally responsible for the quality of the life he or she is now experiencing, and pointing the finger of blame at external forces such as a deity, demons, or fate is not acceptable.

In Buddhism as in Hinduism, the physical universe is a stage for countless rebirths of human beings in a spectrum running from evil to goodness. Nonetheless, there are notable differences between the Hindu and Buddhist interpretations of the transmigration doctrine.

For example, the Buddhist belief system appears to reject the Hindu notion of *atman* (the human soul), an imperishable substance reborn in subsequent lives. In fact, the Buddhist definition of human existence leaves out any reference to a soul. A person is thought to be made up of five distinct elements : (a) a physical body, (b) feelings, (c) the senses,

(d) volition, and (e) consciousness. The union of these five elements, called *Skandhas*, constitutes a personality. Once this union is dissolved, no substantial entity is left.[3] However, a number of passages attributed to Buddha acknowledge the survival and immortality of a part of the personality, which has been variably termed the mind, consciousness, self, or soul:

> The mind takes possession of everything not only on earth,
> but also in heaven, and immortality is its securest treasure-
> trove. (Buddhist Catena, *Anathapindika-Jethavana*)

> The doctrine of the conquest of Self, O Siha, is not taught
> to destroy the souls of men, but to preserve them.
> (*Mahavagga*, VI. 31)

In another text (*Dighna-nikaya*, IV), Buddha defines consciousness (*Vijnana*) as that entity which is "invisible, boundless, all-penetrating, and the ground for *Rupa* (former body), *Vedana* (sensation), *Samjna* (perception), and *Samskara* (will)". The Buddhist element of consciousness or mind appears to replace the Hindu notion of *atman* as the only immortal substance in humans. Yet, in most strands of Buddhism, it is not a person's consciousness that passes over from one life to the next, but his or her *karma*, which leaves its mark on the new existence, just as a seal leaves its mark on wax:

> In respect to rebirth, at the end of one's existence an indi-
> vidual possesses definite characteristics hardened into a kind
> of rigidity; but at the moment of dissolution these character-
> istics are passed over to the soft wax of a new existence in
> another womb. Nothing substantial passes over yet there is
> a definite connection between one complex of elements and
> the next.[4]

Buddha identifies twelve preconditions for stopping this vicious cycle of rebirths. These preconditions form a chain of moral cause and effect in the shape of a circle or wheel (see Illustration 3). Each precondition depends on the one before it. Hence, to stop rebirths, one should begin at the end of the chain and work backward.

The Twelve Preconditions

12. Aging and dying depend on rebirth (if there were no rebirth, then there would be no death).

11. Rebirth depends on becoming (if life X did not die and come to be life Y, there would be no birth of Y).

10. Becoming depends on appropriation (if the life process did not appropriate phenomenal [observable] materials just as a fire appropriates fuel, then there would be no transmigration).

9. Appropriation depends on desire (if one did not thirst for sense objects, for coming to be after this life, and for ceasing to be after this life, then the transmigrant process would not have appropriate fuel).

8. Desire depends on feeling (if pleasant and painful feelings were not experienced, then one would not be conditioned to seek continuing experience of the pleasant or cessation of the unpleasant).

7. Feeling depends on contact (the meaning of sense and object is necessary before pleasure or pain can be felt).

6. Contact depends on the six sense fields (the six pairs of sense and datum – namely, eye/visible form, ear/sound, nose/smell, tongue/taste, body/the touchable, mind/Dharma).

5. The six sense fields depend on name-and-form (mind and body; as the sense fields are equivalent to name-and-form, some lists of the preconditions omit the sense fields).

4. Name-and-form, the whole living organism, depends on consciousness, which here means the spark of sentient life that enters the womb and animates the embryo.

3. Consciousness depends on the dispositions accrued throughout life as karmic residues of deeds, words, and thoughts.

2. The dispositions, or karmic legacy that produces rebirth, depends on ignorance of the Four Holy Truths.

1. Ignorance.[5]

According to this formula, when ignorance ceases, the dispositions end. When dispositions stop, consciousness ceases, and so on until aging and dying are brought to an end. Illustration 3 shows the Buddhist Wheel of Life in its traditional form – held in the mouth and claws of Mara, the demon Death, or Impermanence. The perimeter of the wheel holds the twelve preconditions that cause rebirths. Inside the wheel are the six realms of rebirth, three upper and three lower realms. The three upper realms set aside for the righteous are heaven, the titan realm, and the human realm. The three lower realms reserved for evil-doers are hell, the realm of hungry ghosts, and the animal realm. One's *karma* determines one's next realm of rebirth within the Wheel of Life:

> Truly these beings (endowed with good conduct in body and speech and mind) speak no ill of the Noble Ones: Possessed of right views, they collect the karma of their right views; and after their bodies break up and after they die, they are reborn in a good destiny, in the world of heaven among men. But these beings (endowed with evil conduct in body and speech and mind) speak ill of the Noble Ones: possessed of wrong views, they collect the karma of their wrong views; and after their bodies break up and after they die, they are reborn in an evil destiny, in the realm of hungry ghosts, in the womb of an animal, in hell (the state of woe, and pain and suffering).[6]

The most degraded beings are the inhabitants of hell. Buddhist hells are not, however, eternal. They are purgatorial; once the person has paid for the effects of evil *karma*, he or she will ascend to the human realm. The next lowest realm is the realm of the hungry ghosts. Inhabitants of this realm are condemned to insatiable hunger; they roam the earth, sometimes standing outside city walls and gates, desperately pleading for food. But no one can hear them. Slightly above that is the realm of animals; individuals born as animals are condemned to suffer all the cruelties to which dumb animals are subjected.

The two highest realms of rebirth are heaven (the realm of gods) and the titan realm (the realm of demi-gods). Various beings of good *karma* inhabit these two realms. However, when the traces of their good deeds have run out, they too are subject to reincarnation. The human realm is the lowest in rank among the three upper realms, yet it is the most important realm in the Wheel of Life, for only here one has the opportunity to accumulate good *karma*. The other five realms merely consist of reward or retribution for actions performed in the human realm.

All the six realms, including heaven, are transitory and subject to recurrent death. Therefore, the highest human aspiration, according to Buddha, should be release from continuous rebirths in any of these realms.[7] This release is called *nirvana*, and it lies outside the Wheel because it utterly transcends it. Literally, nirvana means 'blown out,' as of a lamp. When all traces of worldly desires are extinguished in a person, he or she achieves enlightenment or nirvana. Nirvana has also been defined as bliss, the state of freedom from desire, sorrow, and suffering, and escape from the cause-and-effect chain of reincarnation. One can attain nirvana by following the Noble Eightfold Path.

Buddha's Noble Eightfold Path

1. The Right View
Believe the four holy truths:
Existence is suffering.
It is the desire for life and attachment to worldly objects that causes suffering.
Suffering ceases once the desire is expelled.

The path leading to the elimination of desire and consequently to the cessation of suffering is the Noble Eightfold Path.

2. *The Right Intention*
Free your thoughts from lust, worldly desires, untruthfulness, and cruelty to all living creatures.

3. *The Right Speech*
Refrain from lying, harsh language, slander, and idle talk.

4. *The Right Action*
Abstain from killing, stealing, and sexual misconduct.

5. *The Right Livelihood*
Avoid occupations that are harmful to living beings – for example selling weapons, poison or liquor; butchering, fishing, hunting, and so on.

6. *The Right Effort*
Eschew evil thoughts and overcome them.

7. *The Right Mindfulness*
Pay careful attention to every state of the body, mind, and feelings.

8. *The Right Concentration*
Concentrate on one object to bring about special states of consciousness in deep meditation.[8]

Following the Noble Eightfold Path gradually leads to sainthood (arhatship) and eventually to nirvana. The Buddhist saint has overcome the three intoxications of ignorance, sensuality, and craving for rebirth. He has also attained the six perfections – wisdom, morality, charity, forbearance, striving, and meditation. He enjoys higher insight (*Sambodhi*) with its blend of joy, calm, energy, benevolence, and concentration. His happiness is deep as, in the trance of his enlightenment, he has already acquired a foretaste of nirvana. He is the Buddhist ideal of what one should be; he overflows with benevolence, goodwill, and love for humankind. He no longer feels suffering, neither does he take pleasure in earthly joys. He does not wish for death or life. In this state of complete resignation and without any apprehension, he awaits "the putting out of his lamp of life," the entrance into nirvana at death.

The Buddha refused to indicate whether an arhat would exist after death or not. This has led many to view nirvana as an entirely negative state, and some have equated it with 'annihilation.' But that is not what Buddha intended:

> Nirvana seems at first view a completely negative concep-
> tion. It means the end, 'the blowing out,' of suffering exis-
> tence, so that there will be no more transmigration, and
> because the skandhas of the last earthly existence are dis-
> persed and there is no ego remaining over, it would seem
> that Nirvana is 'annihilation.' But the Buddha did not say
> that. He did not think this was true. All he knew, or all he
> cared to say, was that Nirvana was the end of painful
> becoming; it was the final peace; it was an eternal state of
> neither being nor non-being, because it was the end of all
> finite states and dualities. Human knowledge and human
> speech could not compass it.[9]

In the following passage, the Buddha refutes the idea of nirvana as annihilation, and refers to it as simply "the end of suffering":

> Monks, there is that sphere wherein is neither earth nor
> water, fire nor air, it is not the infinity of space, nor the
> infinity of perception; it is not nothingness, nor it is neither
> idea nor nonidea; it is neither this world nor the next nor is
> it both; it is neither the sun nor the moon.
>
> Monks, I say it neither comes nor goes, it neither abides
> nor passes away; it is not caused, established, begun, sup-
> ported: it is the end of suffering.[10]

The Buddha has also given very positive definitions of nirvana. For instance, in one place He defines nirvana as "entirely bliss."[11]

Numerous Heavens and Hells

As noted above, Buddhist eschatology recognizes the existence of a hierarchy of beings who, depending on their *karma*, are continually experiencing different degrees of existence on the Wheel of Life. At any given time, only a tiny minority among us demonstrates the ability to escape the Wheel of Life by entering the state of nirvana. The *karma* of most beings necessitates their rebirth in any of the numerous heavens or hells. Buddhist heavens might be seen as various paradises, while the hells perhaps correspond to the purgatory of the Catholics.

Different schools of Buddhism have varying accounts of what goes on in their heavens and hells. Only one such account can be presented here; this is from the Pali canon. It should be borne in mind that some scholars believe that these accounts are symbolic and should not be taken literally.

Rewards of Heavens

Among the many Buddhist heavens or paradises is the Paradise of Indra. This paradise is full of magnificent vegetation, including trees that change their appearance six times a year during six different seasons. There are other trees that display the dazzling glory of all the six seasons simultaneously, and some that show red and blue lotuses in full bloom. The majestic tree known as the celestial coral tree also grows here. Even musical instruments grow on trees in this paradise. The birds of the Paradise of Indra have "deep-red beaks, crystal eyes, tawny wings tipped with scarlet, and feet half crimson and half white."[12]

There are beautiful celestial maidens here whose playfulness will captivate the ascetics who earned paradise through living austere lives. These maidens are the choicest fruits of the Paradise of Indra; they never age, are always lustful, and are for the enjoyment of anyone who has paid the price in good *karma*. No fault attaches to possessing these maidens. In this hedonistic place, those with good *karma* will live happily, do as they wish, remain young, stay free from any sorrow, and shine with their own light, each according to his own station as determined by his past *karma*.

Compared to this paradise, the earth looks like a cemetery, whose inhabitants are enslaved by distress, old age, and death. However, all the pleasures of the Paradise of Indra are temporary. When the reward of good *karma* runs out, the righteous will fall to earth and wail in deep distress. Buddhist paradises offer no lasting pleasure, freedom, or security. Thus, the ultimate goal of the believer must be total release from the Wheel — nirvana — as no intelligent person would set his heart on temporary relief from sorrow.[13]

Torments of Hells

Often, Buddhist scriptures use very graphic, indeed gruesome, language to describe the plethora of torments that await the wicked in hell. Again, many believe these accounts to be symbolic warnings of the types of unpleasant experiences that the wicked can expect between rebirths. Here is a brief account of some of these torments from the Pali canon:

First, the wardens of hell will drive red-hot iron stakes through the victim's hands, feet, and chest to prevent him from struggling. Then, using sharp razors, they will shave off his flesh, head downwards. Next, they will tie a chariot to his trunk and force him to pull the chariot to and fro across a space blazing with fire. Then he will be forced to climb up and down a fiery mountain of red-hot embers. From here, he is taken into a huge boiler full of melted copper, where he is thoroughly boiled and hurled into the Great Hell where he remains in flames for a long time.

Then one of the four doors of the Great Hell begins to open. All ablaze, the victim runs towards it, but just as he reaches the door it will close before him. He continues to receive various punishments in the Great Hell for some time; then suddenly the eastern door of the Great Hell will open and, this time, the victim will be able to get out.

Unfortunately, though, he now falls into the Hell of Filth, where needle-toothed creatures begin to rip away his flesh and break open his bones so they can eat his marrow. Next, he falls into the Hell of Hot Ashes, then into the great Forest of Sword-Trees where he is made to climb up and down burning trees that are one league high, with spikes half a yard long. From there, the wind pushes him into the neighboring Sword-Leaf-Wood where his hands, feet, ears, and nose are cut off. Next, the victim is plunged into the Caustic River and repeatedly carried up and down the stream.

Finally, using a fish-hook, the wardens pull him out and ask him what he wants now. The poor victim says he is hungry. Upon hearing this, the wardens use a red-hot iron crowbar to open his mouth and shove a red-hot ball of copper down his throat. The wardens then repeat the question. This time, the victim says he is thirsty. Again, they use the red-hot iron crowbar, open his mouth, and pour molten lead into his throat. Next, the wardens push the victim of a hundred tortures back into the Great Hell, where he remains for a long time, until he pays for all the effects of his evil deeds. When the debt is paid, he falls back to earth.[14]

As with its parent religion Hinduism, belief in the twin doctrines of trans-migration and *karma* makes Buddhism very different from western religions. The main theme of Buddhism is that life is suffering, and the best way to eliminate suffering is to achieve detachment from the world and material possessions. However, most people continually fail to become detached, commit evil, and are thus condemned to successive rebirths.

There is a strong belief in the existence of a system of retribution in the universe. All humans receive rewards or punishments for their deeds both on earth and in temporary abodes between rebirths. Among these temporary habitations are numerous heavens and hells. The ultimate goal in life is to escape the Wheel of Life by following the Buddha's Noble Eightfold Path, and to achieve nirvana, a state of total peace, contentment, and detachment. Attaining nirvana is the only way to end earthly suffering and escape perpetual rebirths.

NOTES

1. D. S. Noss. and J. B. Noss, *A History of the World's Religions*, p. 157

2. R. H. Robinson and W. L. Johnson, *The Buddhist Religion: A Historical Introduction (3rd edition)*, p. 38

3. T. Hopkins, *The Hindu Religious Tradition*, p. 56

4. J. B. Noss, *Man's Religions*, p. 158

5. Robinson and Johnson, pp. 16–20

6. Devadutasutta (The messengers of the gods), in *Majjhima-nikaya*, gen. ed. B. J. Kashyap, 3: 250–59, Sutta XXX

7. Robinson and Johnson, pp. 19–20

8. A. Hamilton, (ed.), *Encyclopedia Britannica*, vol. 4., p. 355

9. Noss and Noss, p. 175

10. Udana (Utterances), in *Khuddaka-nikaya*, gen. ed. B. J. Kashyap, ch. VIII, sect. 1–4, pp. 162–63

11. *Milinda-Panha* (The questions of King Milinda), ed. V. Trenckner, pp. 313–26

12. E. Conze, *Buddhist Scriptures*, p. 223

13. Ibid., p. 224

14. Ibid., pp. 224–26

GLOSSARY

Arhat: Buddhist saint (monk) who has followed Buddha's Noble Eightfold Path, released himself from *samsara*, and attained enlightenment and nirvana.

Gautama Buddha: Literally, 'Fully Enlightened One.' The founder of Buddhism (566?–480? BCE).

Karma: The good or evil effect of one's action. The entity of the individual that is carried along to the next rebirth on the Wheel of Life.

Nirvana: Literally, 'blown out.' Has many positive and negative meanings for Buddhists. The positive interpretations include bliss, the unconditioned state of liberation, release from desire, sorrow, and suffering, release from the cycle of birth and death, and extinguishing the cause and effect of reincarnation. The negative meanings include cooled, quenched, and the state of extinction and nothingness.

Noble Eightfold Path: Buddha's blueprint for release from the endlessly turning Wheel of Life (*samsara*) and attaining enlightenment and nirvana.

Realm of Hungry Ghosts: One of the three lower realms on the Wheel of Life reserved for the wicked as karmic retribution. Inhabitants of this realm have an insatiable hunger.

Reincarnation: Rebirth into another body of the same species, particularly human.

Skandhas: 'Heaps/Cluster.' The five temporary elements that give rise to the mistaken sense of 'self.'

Titan Realm: One of the three upper realms on the Wheel of Life. Inhabitants of this realm are demi-gods whose rank is slightly lower than gods.

Transmigration: Similar to but broader than reincarnation; indicates rebirth into any one of six realms within the Wheel of Life.

Wheel of Life: The Buddhist cycle of creation. It highlights the drama of personal choice and its consequences. The Wheel of Life graphically shows how the person is bound to *samsara* (the continuous round of existence).

CHAPTER 5
CHRISTIANITY

INTRODUCTION

Christianity is the religion founded by Jesus of Nazareth, known as Jesus Christ (4 BCE?–29 CE?). Christianity started as a movement within the Jewish religion, but within twenty years of Jesus' death it began to take root among the Gentiles (non-Jews). When Christianity became clearly distinct from the tolerated Judaism, the imperial Roman authorities began to suppress it. Christ Himself was crucified and His early followers were severely persecuted. Many were used as scapegoats on different occasions by the Romans; for instance, Nero blamed Christians for starting the great fire of Rome in 64 CE. Many died martyrs' deaths during that period of turbulence.

Yet despite brutal suppression, the religion began to prosper and to spread across the Roman empire. After three centuries of persecution, in 313 CE the Roman emperor Constantine issued the Edict of Milan, legally tolerating Christianity. In 381, another Roman emperor – Theodosius I – established Christianity as the official religion of the Roman empire.

The main focus of early Christianity was more on Christ's death and resurrection than on His teachings. It was believed that, through Christ's death and resurrection, God had "acted decisively for the salvation of the world, and the kingdom of God announced by Jesus had been inaugurated," states *The Facts on File Dictionary of Religions*.[1] Early Christianity's popularity was partly due to its Gospel, which promised believers immortality, freedom from the power of demons, pardon for sins, personal significance in the sight of God, and a rare brand of fellowship in which discrimination based on wealth, social status, race, or sex had no place. Today, Christianity is the most widespread religion in the world and, by most estimates, has the largest following of any religious system – more than one-and-a-half billion people.

SACRED LITERATURE

The collection of the sacred writings of Christianity is called the Bible (literally, 'Library' or 'Collection of Books'). The Christian Bible comprises two sections which the faithful call the Old Testament and the New Testament. The Old Testament is more or less identical with the Hebrew Bible, with its three division into law, prophets, and writings. In traditional Jewish reckoning, these amount to 24 documents; many Christians add fifteen apocryphal books, which brings the total number of documents in their Bible to 39. The Protestants and modern Catholics do not incorporate these fifteen books into their Bible.

The New Testament contains 27 documents, all written in the century following the crucifixion of Jesus. There are five narrative works (the four Gospels and the Acts of the Apostles), 21 letters (thirteen attributed to St. Paul of Tarsus), and the apocalyptic Book of Revelation.

PERSONAL ESCHATOLOGY

The New Testament has little to say on what happens to individual souls after death. Instead, the major focus of the eschatology of many New Testament books is on *general* eschatology. However, although there is no clear doctrine of personal eschatology in the New Testament, some infer from the parable of Lazarus and the rich man in Luke's Gospel that all the dead go to an intermediate place called Hades. Hades has two compartments that are close to one another yet kept distinctly apart; one is set aside for the righteous, the other for the wicked:

> There was a certain rich man, which was clothed in purple
> and fine linen and fared sumptuously every day:
> And there was a certain beggar named Lazarus, which was
> laid at his gate full of sores,
> And desiring to be fed with the crumbs which fell from the
> rich man's table: moreover, the dogs came and licked his
> sores.
> And it came to pass, that the beggar died, and was carried

by the angels into Abraham's bosom. The rich man also
died, and was buried:
And in hell he lifted up his eyes, being in torments, seeth
Abraham afar off, and Lazarus in his bosom.
And he cried and said Father Abraham, have mercy on me,
and send Lazarus, that he may dip the tip of his finger in
water and cool my tongue: for I am tormented in this flame.
But Abraham said, Son, remember that thou in thy lifetime
receivedst thy good things, and likewise Lazarus evil things:
but now he is comforted, and thou art tormented.
And besides all this, between us and you there is a great gulf
fixed: so that they which would pass from hence to you,
cannot; neither can they pass to us, that would come from
thence. (Luke 16: 19–26)

From this parable, it appears that after death the souls of both the righteous and the wicked would go to Hades to experience either partial recompense or the beginnings of punishment for their conduct on earth.
They both await general resurrection for a final, binding judgment.[2] This
is also indicated in II Peter 2: 4.

A Physical Heaven?

As in Zoroastrianism and some strands of Hinduism and Buddhism, many
of the New Testament's descriptions of heaven and hell have a terrestrial
or physical tenor. In John 14:2 Jesus compares heaven to a house with
many mansions: "In my Father's house, are many mansions; if it were not
so, I would have told you. I go to prepare a place for you."

John, the author of the Book of Revelation, experienced a vision and
in recounting it provides the most detailed biblical account of heaven,
which he calls the holy Jerusalem. However, it is not entirely clear
whether this vision describes a celestial heaven with physical characteristics in the afterlife or, as some Christians believe, an earthly heaven that
will replace the existing earth as the seat of Christ's millennial reign before
the general resurrection of humanity:

And [the holy Jerusalem] had a wall great and high, and had

twelve gates, and at the gates twelve angels, and names written thereon, which are the names of the twelve tribes of the children of Israel.

On the east, three gates; on the north, three gates; on the south, three gates; and on the west, three gates.

And the wall of the city had twelve foundations, and in them the names of the twelve apostles of the Lamb.

And he that talked with me, had a golden reed to measure the city, and the gates thereof, and the wall thereof.

And the city lieth foursquare, and the length is as large as the breadth: and he measured the city with the reed, twelve thousand furlongs. The length, and the breadth, and the height of it are equal.

And he measured the wall thereof, an hundred and forty and four cubits according to the measure of a man, that is, of the angel.

And the building of the wall of it was of jasper: and the city was pure gold, like unto clear glass. And the foundations of the wall of the city were garnished with all manner of precious stones. The first foundation was jasper; the second, sapphire; the third, a chalcedony; the fourth, an emerald; the fifth, sardonyx; the sixth, sardius; the seventh, chrysolite; the eighth, beryl; the ninth, a topaz; the tenth, a chrysoprasus; the eleventh, a jacinth; the twelfth, an amethyst.

And the twelve gates were twelve pearls; every several gate was of one pearl; and the street of the city was pure gold, as it were transparent glass.

And I saw no temple therein: for the Lord God Almighty and the Lamb are the temple of it.

And the city had no need of the sun, neither of the moon, to shine in it: for the glory of God did lighten it, and the Lamb is the light thereof.

And the nations of them which are saved shall walk in the light of it: and the kings of the earth do bring their glory and honour into it.

And the gates of it shall not be shut at all by day: for there

shall be no night there.
And they shall bring the glory and honour of the nations
into it. And there shall in no wise enter into it any thing
that defileth, neither whatsoever worketh abomination, or
maketh a lie: but they which are written in the Lamb's book
of life. (Revelation 21: 12–27)

A Celestial Heaven?

John's vision, as well as Jesus' analogy of heaven as a house and the parable of Lazarus and the rich man, seem to point to an earthly heaven or a
celestial heaven of bodily pleasures, but there are numerous other passages
in the New Testament indicating a celestial heaven inhabited by spirits or
spiritual bodies. For instance, John 18: 36 states that God's kingdom
(heaven) is not of this world. Also, I Corinthians 15: 50 and I Peter 1: 18
note that our physical bodies (flesh and blood) cannot inherit the
Kingdom of God. It would seem inappropriate to ascribe physical attributes to this celestial heaven or kingdom of spirits, and neither would it
make sense to expect material pleasures or rewards for souls in such a
celestial environment. In John 3: 13, Jesus appears to confirm that heaven
is the abode of spirits and spiritual beings: "And no man hath ascended up
to heaven, but he that came down from the heaven, even the Son of man
which is in heaven." In other words, only the spirit that has a celestial origin can ascend to a celestial environment (heaven), and this rule applies
to Jesus Himself (the Son of Man). Passages such as the above have led
some Bible scholars to propose that Jesus' resurrection was not a resurrection of His physical body, which everyone agrees came from Mary's
womb, but of His soul or spiritual body, which came from the celestial
heaven or God's Kingdom.

Resurrection of the Body or Soul?

In Chapter 15 of I Corinthians, Paul discusses the question of resurrection
at length and concludes that only our spiritual bodies can be resurrected
or lifted up to heaven. He refers to his vision of Christ on the way to
Damascus, which resulted in his conversion. What he "saw" was not
Christ's physical body, but the spirit or spiritual body of Jesus. He later
applies the same understanding to what others, including the apostles, had

seen and related of Christ after the crucifixion. In other words, what they too had seen was Jesus' resurrected celestial or spiritual body, not His physical body.

Paul knew that early Christian teachers were having difficulty convincing others that Jesus' resurrection was a physical event, as Luke and John were preaching:

> Now if Christ be preached that he rose from the dead, how
> say some among you that there is no resurrection of the
> dead? But if there be no resurrection of the dead, then is
> Christ not risen. (I Corinthians 15: 12–13)

Paul's solution to the dilemma of resurrection is to propose that we all have a physical body and also a spiritual or celestial existence which is a reflection of all that we sow in this life, an idea somewhat similar to certain Zoroastrian and Hindu notions. In Paul's view, it is this celestial or spiritual body that is raised after death:

> But some man will say, How are the dead raised up? and
> with what body do they come?
> Thou fool, that which thou sowest is not quickened except
> it die: And that which thou sowest, thou sowest not that
> body that shall be, but bare grain; it may chance of wheat,
> or of some other grain:
> But God giveth it a body as it has pleased him, and to every
> seed his own body.
> All flesh is not the same flesh; but there is one kind of flesh
> of men, another flesh of beasts, another of fishes, and
> another of birds.
> There are also celestial bodies, and bodies terrestrial: but the
> glory of the celestial is one, and the glory of the terrestrial is
> another.
> There is one glory of the sun, and another glory of the
> moon, and another glory of the stars; for one star differeth
> from another star in glory.
> So also is the resurrection of the dead. It is sown in corrup-

tion, it is raised in incorruption:
It is sown in dishonour, it is raised in glory: it is sown in
weakness, it is raised in power:
It is sown a natural body, it is raised a spiritual body. There
is a natural body and there is a spiritual body. (I Corinthians
15: 35–44)

Paul's belief that only one's spiritual body ascends to this celestial heaven
is, of course, consistent with what Jesus Himself declared, that only what
has come down from heaven (spirits) can go back to heaven.

A Hell of Fire and Brimstone?

As in most other religions, the abode of the wicked is often portrayed as
a place of fire in Christianity. Matthew characterizes hell as "unquenchable fire" (3: 12), a "furnace of fire" (13: 42, 50), and "everlasting fire" (25:
41) where sinners will receive eternal punishment (26: 46). The Book of
Revelation identifies two places of punishment – hell and a lake of fire and
brimstone (20: 10–15) – for the general resurrection and final judgment.
In Revelation 20: 10–13, the author describes his vision of that time and
place:

> And the devil that deceived them was cast into the lake of
> fire and brimstone where the beast and the false prophet
> are, and shall be tormented day and night for ever and ever.
> And I saw a great white throne, and him that sat on it, from
> whose face the earth and the heaven fled away; and there
> was found no place for them.
> And I saw the dead, small and great, stand before God; and
> the books were opened: and another book was opened,
> which is the book of life: and the dead were judged out of
> those things which were written in the books, according to
> their works.
> And the sea gave up the dead which were in it; and death
> and hell delivered up the dead which were in them: and
> they were judged every man according to their works.

So, while the Hades mentioned in the parable of Lazarus and the rich man is an intermediate place where the righteous and wicked experience pleasure and pain according to their deeds until the general resurrection, hell is reserved for the eternal punishment of wicked souls following the final judgment.

As with heaven, it is not entirely clear what part of the wicked it is that goes to the New Testament hell. Is it their resurrected physical bodies, their souls, or both? Matthew 5: 29–30 quotes Jesus as saying that it is our physical bodies that will suffer punishment in hell:

> And if thy right eye offend thee, pluck it out, and cast it
> from thee: for it is profitable for thee that one of thy mem-
> bers should perish, and not that thy whole body should be
> cast into hell.
> And if thy right hand offend thee, cut it off, and cast it from
> thee: for it is profitable for thee that one of thy members
> should perish, and not that thy whole body should be cast
> into hell.

However, in Matthew 10: 28, Jesus notes that hell is the abode of both soul and body: "And fear not them which kill the body, but are not able to kill the soul: but rather fear him which is able to destroy both soul and body in hell."

Overall, the New Testament's accounts of life after death are very sketchy. One probable reason for this was the conviction of the apostles, who authored most books of the New Testament, that Christ's return was imminent; many among them believed the return would occur within their own lifetimes and trigger humanity's general resurrection and final judgment.

GENERAL ESCHATOLOGY

The final destiny of humankind and dramatic events such as the return of Christ in glory in the hereafter, called the Parousia, are major themes in the Synoptic Gospels (the Gospels of Matthew, Mark, and Luke). Here one finds a number of passages that refer to the return of Christ as an unexpected event preceding the final judgment. In some passages, Christ's return is compared to the breaking in of a thief in the night (Luke 12: 39, Matthew 24: 43), lightning across the sky, the flood in the time of Noah, and the destruction of Sodom (Luke 17: 23–30; Matthew 24: 26–28, 37–41). Mark corroborates this: "But of that day or that hour no one knows, not even the angels in heaven, nor the Son, but only the Father. Take heed, watch, for you do not know when the time will come" (13: 32–33).

While in some passages the Synoptic Gospels present God as the judge of the world, more often it is Christ who is expected to discharge the duties of the judge. For instance, in Matthew's scene of final judgment (25: 31–32) all the nations of the past and present are brought before Christ: "When the Son of man comes in His glory, and all the angels with Him, then He will sit on His glorious throne. Before Him will be gathered all the nations, and He will separate one from the other as the shepherd separates the sheep from the goats."

Christ will use the believers' earthly deeds as the main criterion for judgment: "The Son of man shall come in the glory of His Father with His angels, and then shall he render unto every man according to his deeds" (Matthew 16: 27). The lot of the righteous will be eternal life in the Kingdom of God, while the evil-doer's fate is eternal punishment: "And they [the wicked] will go away into eternal punishment, but the righteous into eternal life" (Matthew 25: 46).

For centuries, Matthew's vision of the Parousia, as well as similar prophecies from Daniel, Isaiah, Ezekiel, Zechariah, and the Book of Revelation, inspired many Christian painters including Michelangelo, Giotto, and Moschos to create remarkable visual representations of the events of the last days. Elias Moschos' "The Last Judgment," completed in 1651, is a stunning example of this (see Illustrations 6 and 7). Here, all the significant events of the second coming of Christ are portrayed in a spectacular icon painting. The focus of this work is the victorious Christ, who stands radiant on the sphere of the universe. Notice the angel supporting the universe; other angels are carrying Christ's aureole, and still others are present to protect Him.

Next to the angels who surround Christ can be seen the kneeling figures of Mary and John the Baptist. The twelve apostles have taken their seats of glory behind Mary and John. In the center of the painting is Hetoimasia, the throne with the open Book of Life in which the deeds of all humanity are recorded. Above Hetoimasia, angels hold the cross as a symbol of Christ's victory over His enemies. Adam and Eve, the first humans, can be seen kneeling before the divine throne. Ezekiel's (37: 1-13) and Daniel's (12: 2) prophecies and St. John's vision (5: 28), which foresaw the trumpet blast by the angels, the subsequent resurrection of the dead, and the sea monsters returning their victims, are portrayed in the middle left.

Terrifying devils continue to torture sinners, whose names are missing from the Book of Life. They are sent to Hades. Numerous devils can be seen trying unsuccessfully to use their claws to grasp the holy souls. They are pushed back into Hades by St. Michael and the angels. The rows of wicked souls are consumed by the open mouth of Hades, which recalls Daniel's vision that "a fiery stream issued and came forth before him" (7: 10).

A long procession of righteous souls can be seen at the lower left. The procession is headed by St. Peter, who is leading the group to the heavenly Jerusalem described in the Book of Revelation. Angels are guarding the gate of the city. Christ, portrayed as high priest, is welcoming the procession with the eucharistic chalice in His hand. Mary is also seen enthroned in paradise as the queen of heaven.

The Fourth Gospel
The Fourth Gospel maintains the eschatological doctrines of the Synoptic Gospels but provides spiritual interpretations for many of the dramatic events associated with the last days. Both Christ's first appearance and His return are considered as judgment times for humankind: "He that believeth not hath been judged already, because he hath not believed on the name of the only begotten Son of God" (3: 18).

Thus, according to John's Gospel, Christ *was* the judgment, even when He appeared in physical form on earth. Those who rejected Him subjected their souls to the wrath of God. Those who believed in Him, on the other hand, were granted everlasting life and Christ's eternal companionship in the afterlife. The Kingdom of God is defined as a condition of the soul after the death of the body. Entering the Kingdom of God simply indicates that one's soul attains eternal life: "He that believeth on the Son hath everlasting life; and he that believeth not the Son, shall not see life; but the wrath of God abideth on him" (3: 36).

The Acts

The Acts consider the return of Christ or the Parousia as impending. What can hasten the Parousia's advent is human repentance:

> Repent ye therefore, and be converted, that your sins may
> be blotted out, when the times of refreshing shall come
> from the presence of the Lord;
> And he shall send Jesus Christ, which before was preached
> unto you. (3: 19–20)

Soon after Christ's return all will be resurrected so Christ can judge them (4: 2). Each individual will receive reward or punishment throughout eternity (10: 42, 17: 31). Finally, the Kingdom of God will be inaugurated at Jerusalem (15: 15–18). All these events were expected hourly at the time of the writing of the Acts.[3]

Judeo-Christian Epistles (I and II Thessalonians)

In I Thessalonians, the exact date of the Parousia is acknowledged to be unknown; nonetheless, Paul appears to expect it to happen during his own lifetime. The Parousia will begin with Christ descending from heaven with a shout. Next, the voice of an archangel and God's trumpet will be heard. The dead in Christ will arise first and be caught up. Then the living, including Paul, will be caught up in the clouds to meet Christ in the air and remain with Him forever (4: 16–18). In II Thessalonians (2: 3), Paul modifies his account of the imminence of the Parousia. Christ's return will be preceded by certain signs: "Let no man deceive you by any means: for that day shall not come except there come a falling away first, and that man of sin be revealed, the son of perdition."

The first event preceding the Parousia, the falling away, was one of the signs of the end in Jewish apocalyptic literature and signified widespread apostasy of the faithful.[4] The second event preceding the Parousia is the appearance of the man of sin – the Anti-Christ – who resides in heaven and reveals himself at the last crisis. He claims to be the Messiah and deceives the faithless by performing miracles; his supreme act of blasphemy is his claim to be God Himself. However, once Christ returns, He slays the Anti-Christ by the breath of His mouth (2: 3–4, 8–10). According to both books of Thessalonians, on the Day of Judgment the doom of the wicked is "eternal destruction" (I Thessalonians 5: 3; II Thessalonians 1: 9), while the righteous will enjoy everlasting fellowship with Christ in the completed Kingdom of God.[5]

The Epistles of the Third Missionary Journey (I and II Corinthians, Galatians, Romans)

Like the Acts, these epistles consider the Parousia to be close at hand (I Corinthians 4: 5; Romans 13: 11, 12). The Parousia is followed by an individual judgment of souls. The two books of Corinthians name Christ as the judge (I Corinthians 4: 4–5; II Corinthians 5: 10). According to Romans, however, it is God who judges humankind *through* Christ (Romans 14: 10). On the Day of Judgment, all souls appear before the seat of judgment, and each renders an account of his or her deeds and is judged accordingly (I Corinthians 6: 9–10; Galatians 6: 7; II Corinthians 5: 10; Romans 14: 12). On that day, the dead are resurrected with spiritual bodies suited for their new spiritual life: "It [the body] is sown in corruption, it is raised in incorruption . . . It is sown a natural body, it is raised a spiritual body" (I Corinthians 15: 42, 44). These epistles also provide rather detailed accounts of the events during the Day of Judgment. For instance, I Corinthians notes that the first group to be raised from the dead on that day will be the righteous souls, who will be given spiritual bodies: "For this mortal nature must put on immortality" (15: 53). Thereupon, Christ gives the kingdom to the Father (15: 24), and all the righteous will live an imperishable life in the Kingdom of God in a new and glorious world where they shall see God face to face.[6]

The Epistles of the Imprisonment (Colossians, Ephesians, Philippians, Philemon)

The letter to Philemon contains no eschatology, and the pastoral epistles

(I & II Timothy and Titus) also have little to say about eschatology. In the other three epistles, terms such as 'salvation' and 'resurrection' are used to indicate the importance for the followers of Christ of leading a spiritual life in both this world and the world to come. By believing in Christ as savior, the faithful receive salvation from sin and are resurrected to holiness in this earthly life. This enables them to enter the kingdom of the Son while still on earth (Colossians 1:13; Ephesians 2: 6; Philemon 3: 20). Having entered the kingdom of the Son, the believer must press on toward the perfect kingdom of the Father:

> Not as though I had already attained, either were already
> perfect: but I follow after, if that I may apprehend that for
> which also I am apprehended of Christ Jesus . . .
> I press toward the mark for the prize of the high calling of
> God in Christ Jesus. (Philemon 3: 12, 14)

The First and Second Epistles of Peter

In Peter's first epistle, the end of all things is considered imminent (4: 7). Although God is generally regarded as the judge (1: 17, 2: 23), it is Christ who will execute the judgment over the living and the dead (4: 5), or over the faithful and the unfaithful (4: 17–18). The righteous will "receive the crown of life" (5: 4) and live a life like that of God (4: 6).

Peter's second epistle says the final judgment will occur at the time of the Parousia. The date of the Parousia is dependent upon human conduct. By living a holy life, a person can hasten its advent (3: 11–12). Upon Christ's return, the present world will be destroyed by fire:

> But the day of the Lord will come as a thief in the night; in
> which the heavens shall pass away with a great noise, and
> the elements shall melt with fervent heat, the earth also and
> the works that are therein shall be burned up. (3: 10)

New heavens and a new earth will be established in place of the old ones (3: 12–13), and Christ's rule on the new earth will begin (1: 11). His only companions in this earthly kingdom will be the righteous (3: 13), as the wicked will be kept under punishment until the Day of Judgment (2: 9), when they will be utterly destroyed (3: 7).

The Book of Revelation

Probably the most explicit and extensive treatment of Christian eschatology can be found in the Book of Revelation, where Christ's millennium receives particular attention. His return to earth is considered certain and imminent, although no definite date is given: "He which testifieth these things saith surely I come quickly: Amen. Even so, come, Lord Jesus" (22: 20).

Interestingly, unlike other New Testament books, in the Book of Revelation the resurrection of the dead is described as having two distinct phases. During each phase different groups of individuals are raised from the dead. The first resurrection occurs shortly after Jesus returns. He first destroys the Anti-Christ and his allies, and then strips Satan of his might and casts him into a bottomless pit where he is imprisoned for a thousand years (20: 1–3).

With the destruction of Christ's archenemies, the first resurrection occurs. During this phase, only Christian martyrs are raised; those brave souls who sacrificed their lives promoting the cause of Christ throughout the centuries are now raised from the dead to share in Christ's glory and rule over the earth for a full thousand years. All other souls remain dead. The Book of Revelation names Jerusalem as the center of Christ's earthly kingdom:

> And I saw the souls of them that were beheaded for the wit-
> ness of Jesus, and for the word of God . . . and they lived
> and reigned with Christ a thousand years.
> But the rest of the dead lived not again until the thousand
> years were finished. This is the first resurrection. (20: 4–5)

At the end of the one thousand years, Satan is released from his prison, and gathering up a huge army, he approaches the center of the messianic kingdom in Jerusalem where the Christian saints and martyrs are established. However, God sends down a fire from heaven which throws Satan's army into confusion and defeat, and Satan himself is thrown into the lake of fire where he is tormented forever (20: 7–10).

The second resurrection then takes place, during which all other individuals are raised to receive recompense for their deeds as written down in the heavenly books. This second resurrection is analogous to the universal resurrection noted in the Zoroastrian, Jewish and Islamic scriptures: "And I saw the dead, great and small, standing before the throne, and the books were opened: and another book was opened, which is the book of life: and the dead were judged out of those things which were written in the books, according to their works" (20: 12).

The wicked are cast into the lake of fire (20: 15), which is the second death for them. The righteous, on the other hand, will dwell in the ideal kingdom of God the Father. Here is the Book of Revelation's description of this seemingly perfect kingdom:

> And I heard a great voice out of heaven, saying, "Behold,
> the tabernacle of God is with men, and he will dwell with
> them, and they shall be his people, and God himself shall be
> with them, and be their God;
> "And God shall wipe away all tears from their eyes; and
> there shall be no more death; neither sorrow, nor crying,
> neither shall there be any more pain: for the former things
> are passed away." (21: 3–4)

The New Testament contains little specific information on the state of the soul after death. However, like most of its doctrines, the personal eschatology of Christianity revolves around the person of Jesus. Perhaps the major contribution of Christian eschatology is the significance it attaches to belief in the person of Jesus as humankind's only hope for salvation. Our eternal bliss or damnation in the afterlife depends on whether we accept or reject Jesus as our personal savior.

Later Christian teaching developed Paul's theology and related Christ's redemptive role to the doctrine of "original sin," which states that, as descendants of the fallen Adam, all men are sinful and deserve eternal punishment. However, in His loving kindness, God sent Jesus – His only begotten Son – to atone for our sins by sacrificing His life for us and dying in our place. Those who choose to believe in this and accept Jesus as their only savior will enter paradise and experience eternal life. Those who reject Jesus are condemned to hell-fire and eternal damnation.

NOTES

1. J. R. Hinnells (ed.), *The Facts on File Dictionary of Religions*, p. 88

2. S. D. F. Salmond, *The Christian Doctrine of Immortality*, p. 345

3. E. C. Dewick, *Primitive Christian Eschatology*, pp. 237–41

4. Ibid., pp. 262–66

5. R. H. Charles, *Eschatology: The Doctrine of a Future Life in Israel: Judaism and Christianity*, pp. 441–45

6. Ibid., pp. 445–47, 454–56

GLOSSARY

Bible: The Christian Bible is the collection of the sacred writings of Christianity. It comprises the Hebrew Bible (Old Testament), fifteen apocryphal books, and the New Testament. In all, the Christian Bible contains 66 books or documents.

Gospels: This term primarily refers to the four first-century records of Jesus' life and teachings. The traditional view considers the authors of these documents to be four of Jesus' apostles, Mark, Matthew, Luke, and John. However, today most Bible scholars question the view that the apostle John authored the fourth Gospel.

Messiah: Jews hoped for the coming of a savior who would deliver them from bondage and return them to their glory days. The term Messiah appears in the apocalyptic literature of Enoch (48: 10), applying to men, particularly kings and high priests. Various Jewish writings of the post-Old Testament era used it to refer to different 'anointed' individuals with special missions who would, in some way, benefit the Jewish people. This included Cyrus the Great, king of Persia.

New Testament: The second part of the Christian Bible, containing 27 documents including the four Gospels, the Acts of the Apostles, 21 letters (thirteen attributed to St. Paul), and the apocalyptic Book of Revelation.

Parousia: Literally, 'presence' or 'coming.' Generally, the Parousia means the return or second coming of Christ, which was expected to happen at any time by most early Christians.

Alternatively, the Parousia has been defined as the event, in the afterlife, of Christ manifesting His true character as the Messiah, unlike His earthly existence when He appeared as a man like others.

Synoptic Gospels: The Gospels of Mark, Matthew, and Luke are collectively called the Synoptic Gospels, perhaps because they present similar views or because they may be read side by side. Today, it is widely recognized that the Gospels of Matthew and Luke are essentially based on the earlier Gospel of Mark.

Illustration 1. *Yama Judges the Dead* (The Maha Avici Hell is shown in the lower segment. Here, there is "suffering without respite.")

Illustration 2. *Zoroastrian Dakhmah (Tower of Silence)* by Trey Yancy

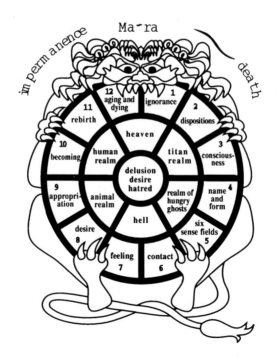

Illustration 3. *Buddhist Wheel of Life* by Trey Yancy

Illustration 4. *The Garden of Eden* by Lucas Cranach, 1530

Illustration 5. *Various Buddhist Hells and their Inhabitants*

Illustration 6. *The Last Judgment* by Elias Moschos

Illustration 7. *The Last Judgment* (detail) by Elias Moschos

بهمه بقیت و دایرهٔ اوپش از عرض زمین و آسمانست و هرچه در آسمانهاست پیش نه
ونظر سوی عرش دار د که تا کی فرمایند که نفخ درصور و مد قوله تعالی و صعق من فی السموا
ت و من فی الارض الامن ش ا تقد عایشه که یدکه از کعب الاحبار شنیدم که کفت از
پیغمبر صلی الله علیه و آله و سلم پرسیدم که اسرافیل کیست فرمود که او ملک یست عظیم و او را
چهار پراست یکی بمغرب را بپوشد و دیکری بمشرق و او را پسیوم سرایل بهمن السماء والار
و جبارم برروی کبیرد از عظمت باری تعالی و سرا و آنجاست که قوایم عرش ست و
پایهای او زیر چشم زمین و درمیان دوچشم او لوحیست از جوهر جون باری تعالی احداثی فرما
قلم را امر فرماید تا بر آن لوح بنویسد پس آن لوح را در میان چشم اسرافیل بدارند و اسرافیل
بجبریل اینها کند صلوات الله علیهما و اعوان اسرافیل بهمه در عالم موجو د آیند و در مولد
وارکان ارواح را در آن بادها نفخ کنند تا حیوان و نبات و معدن شود و فعل ایشان احداث

توتهایی که بدان صلاح و فساد اشیا باشد هذه صوره

Illustration 8. *Archangel Gabriel (Jibril) Blowing his Trumpet*

Illustration 9. *Ascent into the Empyrean* (c. 1500) by Hieronymus Bosch

Illustration 10. *Dante and Beatrice Experience the Beautific Vision* by Gustave Doré (1832–83)

CHAPTER 6

ISLAM

INTRODUCTION

Islam is the religion promulgated by Muhammad (the Praised One). The literal meaning of the term Islam is 'submission' or 'having peace with God.' Muhammad's followers are called Muslims or 'those who submit [to the will of God].' The date of Muhammad's birth is not certain. Most historians agree that He was born between 570 and 571 CE. As a young man, Muhammad often used to visit a cave at the base of Mt. Hira, staying for days at a time. This mountain is situated a few miles north of Mecca in today's Saudi Arabia. Muslim tradition holds that during one of these visits, when Muhammad was around 40 years old, He received the prophetic call from the archangel Gabriel.

Continuing the Judeo-Christian tradition, Muhammad began to preach a monotheistic religion. A decade of opposition from the Meccans eventually forced Him to migrate secretly to Yathrib (Medina) in the year 622 CE. There, He gradually converted the whole city, except the Jews. In a span of a few years, He built an army, defeated the Meccan armies, and became a conquering ruler at the age of 60.

Although Muhammad died in 632, His armies marched on and ultimately conquered parts of three continents. During and following these victories, Muslims steadily built a civilization marked by great advances in various arts, sciences, and literature, which put them far ahead of their European counterparts.

Muhammad is considered by His followers to be both a prophet and a statesman. As a prophet, He proclaimed the oneness of God and brotherhood of the faith. "As a statesman, he was vigorous, astute, determined, and irresistible," according to *An Encyclopedia of Religion*.[1] He won the hearts of His followers and organized them into a compact moral force. Today, the force of His personality continues to have a major impact on the lives of the nearly one billion Muslims around the world.

SACRED LITERATURE

The Qur'án

The Qur'án is the sacred book of Islam, its name deriving from the Arabic word meaning 'to recite.' This signifies to Muslims the importance of frequently reciting the eternal word of God, which they believe was delivered to the prophet Muhammad by the archangel Gabriel. Islamic theologians preach that the Qur'án is the uncreated word of God and pre-existed the world and humanity, and that its archetype, "the Mother Book" or "the Well-Preserved Tablet," was laid up in heaven. Other authoritative revelations that preceded Islam, such as the Jewish and Christian scriptures, are also regarded by many Muslims as genuine transmissions of the "Mother Book," which have been changed and corrupted by humanity and thus do not have the absolute infallibility of the Qur'án.

The term Qur'án was first applied to each revelation announced by Muhammad and then to the whole body of such revelations when they were collected. There are two different traditions regarding the first ever collection of the Qur'án. The first tradition sets the time of the collection during the leadership of the first caliph Abú-Bakr (ruled 632–34 CE), who succeeded Muhammad. The second tradition places the time of the collection during the reign of 'Uthmán, the third caliph, who ruled between 644 and 656 CE.

In its current form, the Qur'án is about the length of the New Testament, and is divided into *súrahs* or chapters revealed in Mecca or Medina; but "many *súrahs* are composite and contain elements from both periods," states *The Facts on File Dictionary of Religions*.[2] Originally, the Qur'án was considered to have been 'released' to the Arabs in their language, but eventually it came to be regarded as a revelation for all humanity, which replaced and superseded the imperfect and corrupt versions of the same heavenly scripture held by the Jews and Christians. As the pre-existent word of God, the Qur'án was for years considered to be untranslatable. Gradually, interlinear translations of the book into other Islamic languages were allowed, and today independent translations of the Qur'án exist in all the major languages of the world.[3]

Hadíth

Literally, the term *hadíth* means 'tradition or saying.' It refers to the body of traditions or sayings attributed to the prophet Muhammad, His companions (reciters of revelations they had memorized before the Qur'án was collected), and other prominent personages in early Islam. The whole body of these traditions constitute the *Sunnah* (Way, Path, or Rule), which is regarded as a source of law, second only to the Qur'án. The *hadíths* complemented the Qur'án by providing guidance on those aspects of law and life on which the Qur'án did not elaborate.

For some time, fabrication of traditions for the purpose of promoting particular sectarian or political doctrines became a flourishing industry. At its peak, an immense corpus of such traditions existed – as many as 600,000. Eventually two scholars, Muhammad al-Bukhárí (810–70) and Muslim ibn al-Hajjáj (817–75), sifted through this enormous mass and reduced the *hadíths* to two collections of about 4,000 each. Most Muslims consider these the "sound collections" or "the two *sahíhs*." Later, four less reliable collections were added to these, and the whole body achieved authoritative status.[4]

PERSONAL ESCHATOLOGY

The fact that the term 'hereafter' (*al-akhira*) occurs 113 times in the Qur'án is indicative of the significance that Islam attaches to the next life. According to the Qur'án, upon death the soul is separated from the body by the angel of death, 'Izra'il. For righteous souls, this separation takes place with ease, but wicked souls are separated from their bodies with violence and commotion (8: 52). Islamic tradition depicts 'Izra'il as an angel with two eyes, one in his face, the other in the nape of his neck. Just before the moment of death, 'Izra'il is said to show himself to the dying, seize the soul without delay, and leave the person's house amidst the cries of the mourners.

Shortly after death, the virtuous person is greeted in the grave by angels with faces as radiant as the sun, while the unbeliever is received by ugly and repulsive creatures. Silk and musk await the righteous, while sackcloth and live coals are in store for the infidel. The believer's grave is transformed into a verdant garden, but the infidel's tomb is laden with seven-headed snakes.

Popular Islamic eschatology retained certain pagan Arab beliefs; for example, just as ancient Hebrews believed all their dead went to an underworld called Sheol or Hades, pre-Islamic Arabs were convinced that the dead had a conscious existence in their graves. Many supplied the deceased with food and drink, and some even pitched tents at gravesides.

Although the Qur'án provides no detailed accounts of the human condition in the grave, the term Barzakh ('grave'/'barrier') occurs in the Qur'án in a number of places (for example, 25: 55, 55: 20, 23: 102). Many Muslim scholars and commentators have taken this to confirm the existence of a state of respite in the grave between physical death and general resurrection, a similar concept to Zoroastrian and Christian accounts.

Later, certain traditions extended the Qur'án's vague references to the life in the grave into a full-blown personal eschatology. Quite possibly, early Muslim theologians and thinkers combined the Zoroastrian belief in a personal judgment in the grave with the pre-Islamic Barzakh doctrine to form a coherent system of personal judgment for the faithful.

One tradition states that, while it is in Barzakh, two fierce-looking black angels with blue eyes, named Nakir and Munkar, will appear to the soul and ask three critical questions: "Who is your God?"; "Who is your prophet?"; and "What is your faith?" In answer to these queries, each soul is expected to identify Alláh as his God, Muhammad as his prophet, and Islam as his faith.[5] If the responses are favorable, the dead's stay in Barzakh will be transformed into a pleasant experience. The grave will be lighted, and its length and breadth will expand seventy times. Under these more tolerable conditions the dead will remain asleep until the general resurrection, when they are reunited with their physical bodies.

On the other hand, if the answers to the angels' questions are not favorable, the tomb begins to close in on the dead person and crush his ribs. A brute who cannot see, hear or speak will begin to torture the dead with an iron whip; as he is deprived of senses, he cannot show any reaction to his victim's cries for help and mercy. Many orthodox Muslims believe that, for

those who fail the Barzakh test, "the punishment of the grave" begins as soon
the funeral party leaves the graveyard, and lasts until the day of resurrection.[6]

Unlike the Hebrew Sheol, therefore, which was static and barren,
Muhammad's underworld is full of energy and movement. It is happy and
joyous for some, but a dreadful place for others.

GENERAL ESCHATOLOGY

Although pagan Arabs had no concept of the resurrection of the body, the
Qur'án also continues the Zoroastrian and Hebrew tradition of belief in a
general bodily resurrection (Ma'ad) and a Day of Judgment for all
humankind. This is despite the fact that Muhammad had much difficulty
convincing fellow Arabs that, some day, God would indeed "gather" their
"bones," "shape" their "fingers," and personally judge them:

> No! I swear by the Day of Resurrection.
> No! I swear by the reproachful soul.
> What, does man reckon We shall not gather his bones?
> Yes indeed; We are able to shape again his fingers. (75: 1–4)

The appointed hour for the general resurrection of humankind is said to
be a secret to all but God; however, a number of signs indicate its
approach. Among the most universally accepted of these signs are the
appearance of the Anti-Christ (Al-Dajjál), the return of Christ, and the
coming of "The Rightly Guided One" (Al-Mahdí).

The Appearance of the Al-Dajjál

According to Shí'ah Muslim tradition, the Al-Dajjál will come from a far-
off island. He is said to be one-eyed and to have the letters KFR, signify-
ing káfir ('infidel') marked on his forehead. He will be a giant, riding a
huge white donkey. The Al-Dajjál will wreak destruction everywhere but
cannot enter Mecca and Medina (the two holiest Muslim cities) for they
are protected by angels. His rule will last 40 days.

The Return of Christ

Forty days into the Al-Dajjál's reign, Jesus will return to earth from heav-

)ajjál, and establish His own kingdom. Christ's rule lasts
be characterized by happiness, love, and prosperity for
ieep and wolves will be seen together; children will play

e of the Al-Mahdí

s held by the Twelver Shí'ahs, who constitute the second-
largest faction of Islam, state that the time of the end and general resurrection of humankind will be preceded by the appearance of another holy
figure – the Al-Mahdí – who will end the reign of oppression and tyran-
ny and fill the earth with justice and equity. A well-known Shí'ah tradition
traces the Al-Mahdí's lineage to the prophet Muhammad Himself and
even gives details of his facial features:

> Abu Sa'id Al-Khurdi reported God's messenger as saying
> "The Mahdí will be of my stock and will have a broad fore-
> head and a prominent nose. He will fill the earth with equi-
> ty and justice as it was filled with oppression and tyranny
> and will rule for seven years."[8]

Another tradition identifies Iran's northeastern province of Khurasan as
the place where the Al-Mahdí first appears: "Thawban reported God's
messenger as saying, 'When you see the black standards come forth from
the direction of Khurasan go to them for God's Khalifa, the Mahdí, will
be among them.'"[9]

Many other signs foreshadow the impending resurrection. Among
them are the appearance of Gog and Magog (18: 93, 21: 96), the rising of
the sun from the west, the coming of the Beast who will brand all men on
their faces so that believers can be recognized from unbelievers, the
smoke which will cover the earth for many days, and the three eclipses in
the east, west, and the Arabian Peninsula.[10] Immediately preceding the
general resurrection are two trumpet blasts by the archangel Isráfíl:

> There shall be a blast on the trumpet, and all who are in the
> heavens and all who are in the earth shall expire, save those
> whom God shall vouchsafe to live. There shall be another

blast on it, and lo! arising they shall gaze around them.
(39: 68).

Some traditions have Isráfíl sounding the trumpet three times. At the first
blast, that of *consternation*, all creatures in heaven and on earth will become
terror-stricken, the earth will shake, mountains will be leveled, the sun will
darken, and the stars will fall. With the second blast, known as the blast
of *examination*, all human beings will expire. This universal death lasts 40
years, and at the end of it there will be torrential rains. Then the third
blast, of *resurrection*, will occur during which all humankind shall be raised
from the dead.[11]

Islam clearly confirms the Zoroastrian and Judeo-Christian belief in
humankind's corporeal resurrection. Both the Qur'án (see 17: 53, 19: 68,
75: 1–5, 101: 1–8) and numerous *badíths* support the notion of physical
resurrection. One *badíth* states that, on the day of resurrection, humanity
will assemble at Jerusalem. The dead will make the journey to Jerusalem
in different ways. Those whose good works have been few will travel to
Jerusalem on foot, and those with whom God is pleased will ride. The infidels will have to crawl all the way to Jerusalem.[12]

Once all humankind arrives at Jerusalem, a period of suspense
ensues, at the end of which God will come down with His angels. Human
beings and angels will assemble before God (Qur'án 25: 24). Each person
will carry his or her own "book" of deeds. Whatever deeds they committed in their lifetimes were recorded in these books by the two Recording
Angels, Kiramun-i-Katibun. The righteous will carry their books of deeds
in their right hands. The wicked will carry theirs around their necks.[13]
Using the book, God will then weigh each person's deeds in special balances (*Mizans*), and the tipping of the scales determines each person's fate:
"Those whose scales [of good deeds] are heavy, they shall be the success-
ful ones. And those whose scales [of good deeds] are light, they are those
who shall lose their souls, abiding in hell" (23: 103–104).

The weighing will take place midway between heaven and hell and
the archangel Gabriel, the intermediary between God and the prophet
Muhammad, will stand by, watching the movement of the scales. When
the judgment is over, all must pass across the Sirat Bridge, which stretches over hell and leads to heaven. Sirat is thinner than a hair and sharper

than a sword. Muḥammad Himself will be the first to cross the bridge in safety. The most righteous will walk across with ease, while the less righteous will have to crawl across. The sinful will labor under a load of guilt and fall into the pit. Some believers will be too frightened to get close to the bridge. Angels will intervene and rescue these souls by helping them cross the bridge through the leaping flames.[14] The purpose and features of the Sirat Bridge are remarkably similar to Zoroastrianism's Chinvat Bridge.

A Paradise Full of Bodily Pleasures?

Life in the Muslim paradise (*al-Jannah*) is full of material delights. It consists of beautiful gardens with streams of wine, milk, and honey (47: 16, 55: 54, 56: 15), with charming tents where lovely damsels (*houris*) abide. The righteous are dressed in exquisite garments (18: 30, 22: 38, 35: 30). Here is a brief description of life in the Muslim paradise:

> Therein they [the righteous] shall recline upon couches,
> therein they shall see neither sun nor bitter cold;
> Near them shall be its shades, and its clusters hung meekly
> down,
> And there shall be passed around them vessels of silver, and
> goblets of crystal,
> Crystal of silver that they have measured very exactly.
> And therein they shall be given to drink a cup whose mixture is ginger,
> Therein a fountain whose name is called salsabil.
> Immortal youths shall go about them; when thou seest
> them, thou supposest them scattered pearls,
> When thou seest them then thou seest bliss and a great
> kingdom.
> Upon them shall be green garments of silk and brocades;
> they are adorned with bracelets of silver, and their Lord
> shall give them to drink a pure draught.
> "Behold, this is a recompense for you, and your striving is
> thanked." (76: 12–22)

The Muslim paradise is specially appealing to the dersert-dwelling Arab who spends most of his lifetime in arid lands; a main feature is flowing water. Two main sources of water are mentioned. One is the Kawthar which has water whiter than milk and sweeter than honey and more fragrant than musk. Some traditions state that the banks of the Kawthar are made of gold and its bed is of pearls and coral. Others claim that the banks of this river are of musk and its bed is of saffron. Then there is the Salsabil, which is a stream or fountain.

Like the Book of Revelation's heavenly Jerusalem, the Muslim paradise is stunningly beautiful. It consists of the most expensive and exquisite precious metals and stones. The walls are made of silver and gold bricks with musk for mortar. The soil is saffron and the gravel is pearls and rubies. In contrast to the vast wastelands of Arabia, whatever the faithful decide to plant in this paradise will grow instantly. All imperfections are removed and all wishes are immediately granted. If the righteous person desires to ride a horse, a ruby horse with wings will appear instantly; if someone looks at the sky and desires a bird, the bird will drop at his feet, roasted and ready;[15] there will be many beautiful maidens. Other traditions, such as the one below, provide additional colorful descriptions of the Muslim paradise:

> He who is least amongst the people of paradise, shall have
> eighty thousand slaves, and seventy two women, and has a
> tent pitched for him of pearls, rubies, and emeralds . . .
> Those who die in the world, young or old, are made of thir-
> ty years of age, and not more, when they enter paradise.[16]

In short, the citizens of the Muslim paradise are treated as kings, and no type of pleasure is denied to them. However, both the Qur'án and the more reliable traditions indicate that the greatest joy awaiting the faithful in paradise is not material but spiritual; it is the joy of beholding Alláh, their creator: "Upon that day faces shall be radiant, gazing upon their Lord" (75: 22).

Muhammad's Journey to Heaven

Muslim traditions include accounts of a supernatural journey by Muhammad to heaven, known as the Mi'ráj or Ascension. Just as some

Christian scholars interpret Jesus' resurrection to be a spiritual event, many Muslim thinkers are convinced that, in reality, Muhammad's ascension was not a physical event but a spiritual one with inner significance. Orthodox Muslims, however, believe in the ascension as a physical occurrence.

While there are different reports of exactly what happened during this journey, most accounts agree that the journey began one night when Muhammad was sleeping near Ka'bah, the sacred building in the middle of the sanctuary at Mecca. Suddenly, the archangel Gabriel appeared, awakened Muhammad, and led Him to the gate of the sacred enclosure. There, a white, winged beast, half-mule, half-donkey, was waiting for the prophet. The prophet mounted the animal and it took Him back to the temple at Jerusalem, accompanied by Gabriel.

At the temple, Muhammad found Abraham, Moses, Jesus, and a company of prophets, whom He led in prayer. Next, two vessels of milk and water were brought for Him. He drank the milk and then Gabriel thus addressed Him: "Muhammad, you have been rightly guided to the *fitra* [the true primordial religion]." Next, a ladder was brought for the prophet, finer than anything He had ever seen; this was the same ladder that the dying see when they are carried to heaven. Muhammad climbed this ladder with Gabriel and passed through the seven heavens. In the first heaven, He saw Adam, the first man, judging the spirits of the dead. He was also shown hell by its keeper, Málík, who temporarily removed its covering to show the prophet the flames of fire that burn the inmates of hell.

In each of the remaining heavens, Muhammad saw great figures of His Hebrew and Judeo-Christian heritage: He saw Jesus and John the Baptist in the second heaven, Joseph the son of Jacob in the third, Enoch in the fourth, Aaron in the fifth, Moses in the sixth, and Abraham in the seventh heaven sitting on a throne at the entrance to paradise.

In the seventh heaven, Muhammad was granted permission to enter paradise, where He went into the presence of God. God commanded Him from that day on to recite 50 prayers a day; this would serve as the distinguishing mark of a pious Muslim. After this face-to-face encounter with God, Muhammad returned to earth. No details of the return journey are given.

The Horrible Pit

Like the pleasures of paradise, the torments of the Muslim hell are also depicted in both the Qur'án and the traditions in terms particularly meaningful to Bedouin Arabs. The Muslim hell or pit has several compartments; the highest of these is called Al-Gehennam, from 'Gehenna' – a Hebrew term first used in the Old Testament. In descending order, the others are "Hell-Fire, the Flame, the Scorcher, the Blazes, the Inferno, and the Abyss, which is bottomless."[17] In these compartments, the wicked will receive varying degrees of punishment, proportionate to the sins they committed on earth. For instance, many will roast in a burning fire and will be given water from a boiling spring. Their food will be foul thorn, which will not satisfy their hunger. They will not be given any cool thing to taste or drink, but will continue to roast on fire, and when their skins are consumed, they will be given new skins so they can suffer fresh torments: "Surely those that disbelieve in our signs, We shall certainly roast them at a fire; as often as their skins are wholly burned, We shall give them in exchange new skins, that they may taste the chastisement" (4:59). For other Qur'ánic references to hell and its horrors, see 7: 178, 46: 40, 50: 29, 72: 15, 78: 21–30, and 89: 24.

One tradition states that God will make the bodies of infidels larger so they will suffer more. They will be bitten by scorpions as large as mules and by serpents as big as camels. They will have huge long tongues, mouths vomiting blood, and entrails filled with fire. They will be entrapped in stinking rivers full of vile creatures. All will be tortured by fire, but the degree of punishment differs depending on one's sins.[18]

Unlike the Christian accounts, however, where all the wicked are condemned to hell forever, only two groups are eternal inhabitants of the Muslim hell. These are the idolater (*mushrik*) who ascribes plurality to God, and the infidel (*kafir*) who has turned away from Islam: "Whosoever of you turns from his religion, and dies disbelieving, . . . those are the inhabitants of fire; therein they shall dwell forever."[19] The strong condemnation of idolatry in Islam is probably due to the long history of Arab paganism and perhaps a reaction to the Christian doctrine of the Trinity, which Muslims consider polytheistic. Turning away from Islam is also regarded as highly blameworthy because Muhammad's religion is considered to be the latest and most complete revelation of God's Word.

The Zoroastrian Heritage

Even a cursory look at Muslim eschatology reveals numerous similarities between Muslim and Zoroastrian accounts of the afterlife. Many of these are attributable to the Arab conquest of Persia and the subsequent impact of Zoroastrian eschatology on that of Islam. Here are some of those similarities:

The State of the Soul before Judgment

According to Later Avestan Texts and Pahlavi literature, after death the soul spends three days and three nights near the body before undergoing individual judgment. During this period, the righteous soul experiences happiness, while the wicked soul suffers anguish. In Islam, immediately after death the soul stays in Barzakh (a respite state in the grave) where it is interrogated by the two angels of death. If the soul passes the Barzakh test, it will enjoy happiness; otherwise, it will endure torment until the general resurrection of humankind.

The Two Judgments

There are two judgments in both Zoroastrianism and Islam: an individual and a universal judgment. In Zoroastrianism, the individual judgment occurs at the Chinvat Bridge, while in Islam it takes place in the grave with the two interrogating angels. In both religions, a universal judgment occurs at the end of time.

Interestingly, Islam's universal judgment appears to borrow from the Zoroastrian individual judgment. In both cases, the deeds of the soul are measured in special balances and the fate of the soul is determined by the tipping of the scales. However, while in Zoroastrianism the judge is either Zoroaster (as in the Gathas) or a triad of heavenly judges (as in the Later Avestan Texts and Pahlavi literature), in Islam the judge is always Alláh.

The Bridge

Both religions maintain that the righteous and wicked must all cross a bridge stretching over hell and leading to heaven. This bridge, called Chinvat in Zoroastrianism and Sirat in Islam, widens for the righteous so they can cross it easily and reach heaven; but it turns razor sharp for the wicked, forcing them to slip and fall into hell.

Heaven and Hell

In both religions, the notions of heaven and hell exist, but in Zoroastrianism these places are temporary abodes until the final rehabilitation, while in Islam hell is the permanent dwelling-place of idolaters and infidels.

Vision of the Creator

The greatest joy of the righteous in heaven is experiencing a meeting with the creator. Zoroastrian belief systems call this figure Ahuramazd, while Islam gives Him the title Alláh.

The afterlife is one of the major themes of the Qur'án and Muslim traditions. Earthly life is regarded as a preparatory stage for the life to come. Islam continues the Zoroastrian and Hebrew traditions of belief in a personal judgment for individual souls and a general judgment for humanity in the fullness of time, and also preserves the tradition of a heaven of physical delights and a hell of physical tortures. However, to make the Muslim retribution system relevant, Islam relates the pleasures of its paradise to the desires of Arab desert dwellers, and the punishments of its hell to their fears.

NOTES

1. V. Ferm (ed.), *An Encyclopedia of Religion*, p. 501

2. J. R. Hinnells (ed.), *The Facts on File Dictionary of Religions*, p. 264

3. Ibid.

4. Ibid., p. 140

5. C. J. Bleeker and G. Widengren, *Historia Religionum*, vol. II, p. 185

6. Ibid.

7. H. Masse, *Islam*, p. 136

8. J. Williams, *Themes of Islamic Civilization*, p. 195

9. Ibid.

10. A. Jeffry, *Muḥammad & His Religion*, p. 144

11. T. P. Hughes, *Dictionary of Islam*, pp. 540–41

12. Ibid., p. 541

13. Bleeker and Widengren, p. 186

14. A. Toynbee et al., *Life After Death*, p. 128

15. Ibid., p. 130

16. Hughes, p. 453

17. Toynbee et al., p. 129

18. Hughes, p. 453

19. J. Smith and Y. Haddad, *The Islamic Understanding of Death and Resurrection*, p. 86

GLOSSARY

Abyss: The lowest of hell's compartments, which is bottomless.

Al-Dajjál: The Anti-Christ whose appearance is a sign of the impending general resurrection of humankind.

Al-Gehennam: The highest of hell's compartments.

Al-Jannah: Paradise or heaven.

Alláh: God.

Al-Mahdí: Literally, 'the Rightly Guided One.' The Promised One of Muslims who will appear before the general resurrection of humankind to end oppression and fill the earth with justice and equity.

Barzakh: Literally, 'grave.' A pagan Arab concept adopted by Muslims which led to the belief in a respite state of existence in the grave, between physical death and general resurrection. Certain Islamic traditions suggest a personal judgment for individuals during their stay in

Barzakh.

Blazes: One of the lower middle compartments of hell.

Flame: The third highest compartment of hell.

Gabriel: The archangel of revelation in Islam. He is believed to have brought God's revelation to Muhammad.

Gog and Magog: The enigmatic duo mentioned in Ezekiel's apocalyptic vision of the final assault on the forces of evil before the establishment of God's kingdom. Post-Old Testament rabbinic Jewish literature identifies Gog and Magog as rebels who will oppose God and His anointed one.

Hadíth: The body of traditions or sayings attributed to Muhammad, his companions, or other prominent early Muslims. While the Qur'án is considered the primary source of Islamic divine law, the *hadíths* constitute a secondary source which usually deals with Islamic customs and codes of behavior. Thus the *hadíths* complement and explain the Qur'án.

Hell-Fire: Next to the highest of hell's compartments.

Inferno: Next to the lowest of hell's compartments.

'Izra'il: The archangel of death.

Káfir: 'Infidel'. A Muslim who turns away from his religion; one of only two groups condemned to hell for ever. See also *Mushrik*.

Kawthar: A river in paradise with water whiter than milk and sweeter than honey. The banks of the Kawthar are said to be either of gold or musk and its bed of pearls and coral or saffron.

Kiramun-i-Katibun: The two Recording Angels who record every action of every person in his or her own book of deeds which God will use to pass a final judgment during general resurrection.

Ma'ad: Humankind's physical resurrection at the end of the world, when all individuals will be judged by God and sent to either heaven or hell.

Mi'ráj: 'Ascension.' The night journey of Muhammad to the seven heavens and paradise.

Mizans: Special balances God will use after the general resurrection to weigh the deeds of each person as recorded in their individual 'books' of deeds.

Mushrik: 'Idolater.' One who ascribes plurality to God. The idolater and the infidel are the only groups who can never hope to get out of the Muslim hell.

Nakir and Munkar: The two fierce-looking black angels with blue eyes who, after the death of the body, will appear to the deceased in the grave and ask him to identify his God, his prophet, and his faith. In answer, he is expected to identify Alláh as his God, Muhammad as his prophet, and Islam as his faith.

Qur'án: The sacred book of Islam. Muslims consider it the pre-existent, eternal word of God, delivered to the prophet Muhammad by the archangel Gabriel. It is the repository of Islamic divine law. The term first applied to individual revelations reported by Muhammad and, later, to the whole body of such revelations first collected during the reign of either the first caliph, Abú-Bakr, or the third caliph, 'Uthmán.

Salsabil: A stream or fountain in paradise.

Scorcher: The middle compartment of hell.

Sirat: Literally, 'path'. This is the bridge that stretches over hell and leads to heaven. It is thinner than a hair and sharper than a sword. The righteous will cross it with ease and reach heaven, while infidels will slip and fall into hell.

CHAPTER 7
THE BAHÁ'Í FAITH

INTRODUCTION

The Bahá'í Faith is the newest and probably the least well-known world religion discussed in this book. Yet according to the 1992 *Britannica Book of the Year*, only Christianity has spread to more countries and territories than this 150-year-old faith.[1] The prophet-founder of the Bahá'í Faith was Mírzá Husayn 'Alí of Núr (1817–92 CE), known as Bahá'u'lláh or the 'Glory of God.' The term Bahá'í means follower of Bahá or 'Glory.' So, as the followers of Christ are called Christians, the followers of Bahá'u'lláh are called Bahá'ís.

Basic Teachings
Among the pivotal principles of this faith are a belief in the oneness of God, the oneness of religion, and the oneness of humanity. By the oneness of God it is meant that there is only one creator, who has been given different names throughout religious history (e.g. Brahman, Ahuramazd, Yahweh, the Uncreated, Father, Alláh, God). Bahá'u'lláh also taught the oneness of religion, that is, all the major religions have the same divine origin and teach the same fundamental truths. Thus, to Bahá'ís, all the other religions covered in this book are representations of the one and only religion that God has ever taught. The names of these religions and the messengers who founded them are different but they all are part of God's eternal plan, with the major goal of spiritual transformation for humankind:

> The Prophets and Messengers of God have been sent down
> for the sole purpose of guiding mankind to the straight Path
> of Truth. The purpose underlying their revelation hath been
> to educate all men, that they may, at the hour of death,
> ascend, in the utmost purity and sanctity and with absolute
> detachment, to the throne of the Most High.[2]

With every revelation, humankind has moved toward greater degrees of unity and higher levels of civilization. Human history provides ample evidence for this, as we have seen steady movement from family unity to the establishment of villages, towns, cities, states, nations, empires, alliances, and now international organizations. Bahá'u'lláh taught the oneness of humanity, which means that all people, regardless of race, color, sex, ethnicity, nationality, language, or culture, are members of one big family – the human family.

Another central teaching of the Bahá'í Faith is the concept of *progressive revelation*. To Bahá'ís, religious truth, much like scientific truth, is relative. Thus, throughout history, humankind has received guidance from various prophets that is appropriate to its spiritual, intellectual, geographical, and socio-cultural capacity. Hence, many of the variations we see among divine religions are, to Bahá'ís, simply attempts by a loving creator to tailor the same message of unity, love and brotherhood to the requirements of an evolving humanity in a particular time and place.

The Bahá'ís believe that the phenomenal progress humanity has witnessed in the past 150 years is directly attributable to the appearance of their prophet, Bahá'u'lláh, whom they consider the Lord of this age, and the spiritual energy He has released. This spiritual energy will, after an initial period of turmoil, lead to the unification of all the people on this planet and the ushering in of the golden age of humanity, bringing unprecedented spiritual and material progress.

A by-product of the belief in progressive revelation is that, as humanity's intellectual and spiritual capacity grows and we move toward greater degrees of unification, so does our ability to understand complex religious and metaphysical phenomena. This faith therefore provides an extensive discussion of the afterlife.

Bahá'í View of the Nature of Humanity
The Bahá'í Faith maintains that humans are essentially spiritual beings who undergo a temporary physical experience on this planet. Along with a physical body, each human being possesses a rational soul (spirit) which is the core of his or her being and is vouchsafed by a loving creator. This rational soul consists of a single, indivisible, non-material substance and is indestructible. Understanding the crucial difference between the sub-

stance of the human soul and the various physical entities in our universe is vital to an understanding of Bahá'í eschatology. Bahá'u'lláh's son, 'Abdu'l-Bahá, explains this:

> The whole physical creation is perishable. These material bodies are composed of atoms; when these atoms begin to separate decomposition sets in, then comes what we call death. This composition of atoms, which constitutes the body or mortal element of any created being, is temporary. When the power of attraction, which holds these atoms together, is withdrawn, the body, as such, ceases to exist.
>
> With the [human] soul it is different. The soul is not a combination of elements, it is not composed of many atoms, it is of one indivisible substance and therefore eternal. It is entirely out of the order of the physical creation; it is immortal.[3]

The human soul establishes connection with the physical body at the moment of conception. This body serves as a vehicle for the soul in its physical experience on earth. Yet the higher nature of the soul as a single and indivisible substance makes it independent of the body to which it is connected. Thus, death or the decomposition of that body will have no impact upon the life of the soul, which is not made up of matter. This indestructible substance continues to live eternally in the limitless realms of God. The Bahá'í writings describe the human soul as the seat of one's personality and conscience.

The main reason our soul goes through a physical existence on this planet is so it can develop its spiritual potential.[4] This can be attained only through the knowledge and love of God and reflection of the divine attributes that are potentially present in each soul. As there can be no direct communication between the Absolute (God) and His finite creation, human beings can learn about their creator only through special beings who act as intermediaries. These are the prophets or, to use Bahá'í terminology, the manifestations of God. This term is used to refer to Bahá'u'lláh as well as to all the other prophets of the past, including those mentioned in previous chapters of this book. These manifestations have both a human and a divine side. Their divine side is like a flawless mirror that fully reflects God's perfections. On their human side, they are ordinary people subject to the same limitations and frailties as everyone else. However, these beings only temporarily take on human form to facilitate communication with humanity; their essence is of a higher substance: "The source of all learning is the knowledge of God, exalted be His Glory, and this cannot be attained save through the knowledge of His Divine Manifestation."[5]

Once we attain knowledge of God through the manifestation appropriate to our age, we can focus on the development of our souls, which involves a continuous attempt to reflect the attributes of God that are within us: "The purpose of the one true God, exalted be His Glory, in revealing Himself unto men is to lay bare those gems that lie hidden within the mine of their true and inmost selves."[6]

Bahá'í writings state that humanity is created in God's image and thus potentially possesses the divine attributes and perfections of the creator. To reflect these hidden virtues, one needs to polish the mirror of one's heart. The task of divine manifestations is to guide people in accomplishing this goal:

> Through the teachings of this Day Star of Truth [the manifestation] every man will advance and develop until he attaineth the station at which he can manifest all the potential forces with which his inmost true self hath been endowed. It is for this very purpose that in every age and dispensation the Prophets of God and His Chosen Ones have appeared amongst men, and have evinced such power as is born of God and such might as only the Eternal can reveal.[7]

To Bahá'ís, the surest means of attaining true and lasting happiness both in this world and in the worlds to come is to focus on the prime purpose of one's existence, namely spiritual progress. This is an eternal journey starting here on earth and, after physical death, continuing in the infinite spiritual worlds of God.

Life as Preparation

Although the Bahá'í Faith puts much value on this life, has an agenda for the establishment of a just and humane social order, and considers the unity of humankind as its pivotal mission, its sacred scriptures constantly remind the faithful of the transitory nature of earthly life and describe it as a preparatory stage for a higher spiritual form of existence in loftier realms. Physical experience on this planet is described as the embryonic preparation for an eternal spiritual life which follows the death of the body.

A favorite Bahá'í analogy compares our life and spiritual progress on earth to the life and development of the fetus in the womb. The fetus spends about nine months in the womb preparing for entry into this world. During that period, it develops limbs, eyes, ears, and other physical features essential for its earthly existence. In the same manner, this terrestrial world is a place where each individual can acquire the spiritual means that are essential for existence in the next world. The crucial difference is that while physical development in the mother's womb is involuntary, the spiritual development possible in this world is solely dependent upon conscious individual effort:

> Know thou that all men have been created in the nature
> made by God, the Guardian, the Self-Subsisting. Unto each
> one hath been prescribed a pre-ordained measure, as
> decreed in God's mighty and guarded Tablets. All that
> which ye potentially possess can, however, be manifested
> only as a result of your own volition.[8]

As the next worlds are spiritual in nature, the qualities required for existence and operation there must necessarily be spiritual. These are the knowledge and love of God and the ability to reflect His virtues. 'Abdu'l-Bahá explains this:

> If he [man] possesses the knowledge of God, becomes ignit-
> ed through the fire of the love of God . . . becomes the
> cause of love among mankind and lives in the utmost state of

sanctity and holiness, he shall surely attain to second birth, be baptized by the Holy Spirit and enjoy everlasting existence.[9]

SACRED LITERATURE

The Bahá'í revelation comprises the vast body of writings of Bahá'u'lláh in the form of books and letters, which are estimated to amount to over 100 volumes if compiled. Bahá'ís regard these as sacred. Almost all of these works were written in Persian and Arabic; the most important have been translated into English and many other languages. The writings and recorded talks of 'Abdu'l-Bahá, Bahá'u'lláh's eldest son and appointed successor, have a derived but equally binding authority and are also considered to be holy scripture. Bahá'ís also regard as holy scripture the sacred texts of other major world religions, including the Bible and the Qur'án.

Bahá'í sacred texts cover a very diverse range of subject matter, covering basic concepts of the religion, principles of human life and conduct, laws and ordinances, and guidelines for the establishment of social and administrative institutions. Among the most important works in Bahá'í scripture are the following:

The Works of Bahá'u'lláh

The Most Holy Book (Kitáb-i-Aqdas)
As its name suggests, this is one of Bahá'u'lláh's most important works, containing most of His laws and ordinances on such subjects as prayer, fasting, marriage, divorce, inheritance, pilgrimage, the obligation to work, and such prohibitions as slavery, mendicancy, gambling and the use of drugs, which Bahá'ís, collectively and individually, are to follow.

The Book of Certitude (Kitáb-i-Íqan)
In this work Bahá'u'lláh sets out the basic concepts of His revelation. Here He delineates the principle of progressive revelation, proclaiming the oneness of God, the station of His messengers as 'mirrors' through whom humanity can obtain knowledge of God, and the unity of their divine teachings, and provides spiritual interpretations for a number of abstruse passages in the Qur'án and the Bible.

Gleanings from the Writings of Bahá'u'lláh
This book contains a selection of Bahá'u'lláh's most important works, many of them still unavailable in English in their full form, on the purpose of religion, the spiritual nature of humanity, and the transformation of human society.

The Hidden Words
This short work focuses on the principles of human life and conduct and contains Bahá'u'lláh's exhortations and admonitions to humanity, as well as His explanations of the nature and purpose of life, humanity's unique place in the world of creation, and the mysterious relationship between humankind and God.

The Seven Valleys
Written in response to questions from a prominent súfí of the time, this allegorical treatise utilises the terminology and form familiar to those who were acquainted with Islamic mystical literature. Here Bahá'u'lláh identifies the seven stages or valleys a true seeker after the truth must pass through in his or her quest for the Beloved (God).

The Works of 'Abdu'l-Bahá

Selections from the Writings of 'Abdu'l-Bahá
This is the most important collection of the letters of 'Abdu'l-Bahá in which he elucidates the teachings of the Bahá'í Faith on a wide range of issues from spiritual questions to marriage and child education.

Some Answered Questions
This is one of the best-known collections of the talks of 'Abdu'l-Bahá. It consists of replies to a wide range of spiritual and philosophical questions, and its themes range from the role and impact of prophets in human history to biblical subjects and Bahá'í theology and metaphysics, such as the origin of the universe, the immortality of the soul, and the question of evil.

Paris Talks
This small volume consists primarily of the informal talks 'Abdu'l-Bahá

gave during a nine-week stay in Paris, France in 1911. Given in Persian and translated into French for the audiences, they focused on one or more of Bahá'u'lláh's central teachings and ranged from metaphysical questions on the nature of the soul to social issues such as the causes of war and the need for universal peace.

PERSONAL ESCHATOLOGY

The Bahá'í Faith considers the human soul to be immortal and capable of making progress after its temporary connection with the body is severed:

> Know thou of a truth that the soul, after its separation from the body, will continue to progress until it attaineth the presence of God, in a state and condition which neither the revolution of ages and centuries, nor the changes and chances of this world, can alter. It will endure as long as the Kingdom of God, His sovereignty, His dominion and power will endure.[10]

Unlike in the material realm where the soul's development is dependent on our own conscious efforts, the progress of the soul in spiritual realms depends upon different means. First and foremost among these is the grace and bounty of God. Additional means include the intercession and sincere prayers of others and good deeds performed by others on earth in the name of the departed person:

> The grace of effective intercession is one of the perfections belonging to advanced souls, as well as to the Manifestations of God. Jesus Christ had the power of interceding for the forgiveness of His enemies when on earth; and He certainly has this power now . . . Followers of the prophets have also this power of praying for the forgiveness of souls. Therefore, we may not think that any souls are condemned to a stationary condition of suffering or loss arising from absolute ignorance of God. The power of effective intercession for them always exists.[11]

Through these means, the human soul is capable of making infinite progress in the countless worlds of God. Nonetheless, the progress of the soul can only be within its own condition (the condition of servitude). Bahá'í literature identifies three conditions of existence: the conditions of deity, of prophethood, and of servitude, and human souls always exist in the condition of servitude, regardless of the amount of progress they make. By nature and substance, human beings do not have the capacity to move up to the higher realms of existence, but they can make infinite progress in the plane of servitude.[12]

The State of the Soul Immediately before and after Death

Bahá'u'lláh states that a person begins to experience a sense of reward and punishment immediately *before* death. For instance, those who have neglected their spiritual development shall "when breathing their last be made aware of the good things that have escaped them, and shall bemoan their plight, and shall humble themselves before God. They shall continue doing so after the separation of their souls from their bodies."[13]

In another passage, Bahá'u'lláh states that immediately after death, spiritually developed souls shall experience indescribable joy, whereas erring souls will be seized with fear and confusion:

> It is clear and evident that all men shall, after their physical
> death, estimate the worth of their deeds, and realize all that
> their hands have wrought. I swear by the Day Star that
> shineth above the horizon of divine power! They that are
> the followers of the one true God shall, the moment they
> depart out of this life, experience such joy and gladness as
> would be impossible to describe, while they that live in
> error shall be seized with such fear and trembling, and shall
> be filled with such consternation, as nothing can exceed.[14]

Nonetheless, undeveloped souls are not barred from redemption. They can continue to make progress in the next world by a variety of spiritual means including God's forgiveness and prayers and intercession by others and even by themselves: "Undeveloped souls must gain progress at first through the supplications of the spiritually rich; afterwards they can progress through their own supplications."[15]

Rewards and Punishments of the Next World

According to the Bahá'í writings, a soul's retribution or recompense in the next world is entirely spiritual. While they are replete with references to reward and punishment, and heaven and hell, the descriptions they offer differ from those of past scriptures. For Bahá'ís, the rewards of the next world are closeness to God, attaining eternal life, acquiring divine perfections, and receiving spiritual bounties and everlasting felicity. Similarly, the punishments of the afterlife are remoteness from God and being deprived of His spiritual blessings and bounties.[16]

Bahá'u'lláh does not appear to confine the rewards of the next world solely to His own followers. Instead, when describing the true believer, He uses broader terms such as "every pure, every refined and sanctified soul."[17]

Heaven and Hell

The Bahá'í Faith regards conventional descriptions of heaven and hell as physical places of material delights or punishments as symbolic. The Bahá'í belief that the human soul is non-material leaves no room for a literal interpretation. In fact, the Bahá'í writings teach that it is the non-material nature of the soul that guarantees its survival and immortality. This also frees the soul from subjection to the physical limitations of material objects such as the need for a given 'time' and 'place' for existence. Only beings with physical properties are in need of time and place as we know them on earth. Since the soul is not made up of matter, it is not in need of time or place as we define them; once freed from connection to a material body, the soul will gain greater knowledge of God, its own essence, and the mysteries of creation, and will gain a degree of omnipresence.

Instead of physical places, the Bahá'í writings describe heaven and hell as "spiritual conditions." Heaven is defined as spiritual closeness to God's manifestation, while hell is spiritual remoteness from the manifestation. God Himself is sanctified from any limitations including "closeness" and "remoteness." Bahá'í definitions of heaven and hell also apply to the conditions and experiences that the soul undergoes while still on earth;

heaven is defined as the joy of knowing and loving God and attempting to draw closer to Him by following the teachings of the messengers of God and acquiring divine attributes. A person who does this lives in the heaven of God's good pleasure while on earth and, after death, attains everlasting life. Hell, on the other hand, lies in deprivation of the knowledge of God and failure to draw close to Him. Although all souls continue their existence in the afterlife, the quality of life of a soul who has little or no knowledge of God is as death compared to the quality of life of pure and sanctified souls.

Nature of the Life of the Soul in the Next World

The true nature of the future life of the soul is beyond anything we can comprehend or experience on this physical plane. Bahá'u'lláh states that it is not appropriate for Him to divulge the whole character of the life of the soul after death:

> The nature of the soul after death can never be described,
> nor is it meet and permissible to reveal its whole character
> to the eye of men . . . The world beyond is as different from
> this world as this world is different from that of the child
> while still in the womb of its mother.[18]

In a number of other passages, Bahá'u'lláh explains why he should not reveal the secrets of the afterlife:

> The mysteries of man's physical death and of his return [to
> the Creator] have not been divulged, and still remain
> unread. By the righteousness of God! Were they to be
> revealed, they would evoke such fear and sorrow that some
> would perish, while others would be so filled with gladness
> as to wish for death, and beseech, with unceasing longing,
> the one true God – exalted be His glory – to hasten their
> end.[19]

> If any man be told that which hath been ordained for such a
> soul [the pure, refined, and sanctified soul] in the worlds of

God, the Lord of the throne on high and of earth below, his
whole being will instantly blaze out in his great longing to
attain that most exalted, that sanctified and resplendent
station.[20]

Nevertheless, the Bahá'í writings contain certain allusions to the nature of
the soul's life in the next worlds. For instance, Bahá'u'lláh states that first
the soul will take on a special form worthy of its condition and new habitation: "When the soul attaineth the Presence of God, it will assume the
form that best befitteth its immortality and is worthy of its celestial habitation."[21] 'Abdu'l-Bahá also indicates that the soul will retain its consciousness and individuality and remember its physical life on earth; it will
recognize other souls and engage in communion with them. However,
this communication is purely spiritual:

And know thou for a certainty that in the divine worlds the
spiritual beloved ones will recognize one another, and will
seek union with each other, but a spiritual union. Likewise, a
love that one may have entertained for anyone will not be
forgotten in the world of the Kingdom, nor wilt thou forget
there the life thou hadst in the material world.[22]

'Abdu'l-Bahá further elaborates on this:

Undoubtedly, the holy souls who find a pure eye and are
favored with insight will, in the kingdom of lights, be
acquainted with all mysteries, and will seek the bounty of
witnessing the reality of every great soul . . . Likewise will
they find all the friends of God, both those of the former
and recent times, present in the heavenly assemblage.[23]

Marital bonds in this world will also survive physical death, if the bond
has a spiritual foundation. However, in the absence of gender limitations,
the relationship between the souls will be purely spiritual. Direct communication with God will remain impossible in the next life but the soul will
gain new spiritual insights by conversing with "prophets of God and His

chosen ones."[24] Also, "The mysteries of which man is heedless in this earthly world, those he will discover in the heavenly world, and there will he be informed of the secret of truth."[25]

The Realm of Souls

'Abdu'l-Bahá asserts that the realm of the souls is within our world because the entire order of existence is a single world:

> If ye ask as to the place, know ye that the world of existence is a single world, although its stations are various and distinct . . . Those souls who are pure and unsullied, upon the dissolution of their elemental frames, hasten away to the world of God, and that world is within this world. The people of this world, however, are unaware of that world, and are even as the mineral and the vegetable that know nothing of the world of the animal and the world of man.[26]

Bahá'í writings acknowledge the existence of a hierarchy of souls in the afterlife. The merits and accomplishments of each soul determine its place in this hierarchy. Souls of lower achievements cannot fully grasp the station and accomplishments of those above them:

> They [the souls] that are of the same grade and station are fully aware of one another's capacity, character, accomplishments and merits. They that are of a lower grade, however, are incapable of comprehending adequately the station, or of estimating the merits, of those that rank above them. Each shall receive his share from thy Lord.[27]

In another passage, 'Abdu'l-Bahá gives the following analogy to illustrate the quality of life of various souls in the next life:

> For example, the eye and the nail are living; but the life of the nail in relation to the life of the eye is nonexistent. This stone and this man both exist; but the stone in relation to the existence of man is nonexistent . . .

> In the same way, the souls who are veiled from God, although they exist in this world and in the world after death, are, in comparison with the holy existence of the children of the Kingdom of God, nonexisting and separated from God.[28]

Attaining the Presence of God

The Bahá'í Faith considers God's essence to be transcendent and incomprehensible to the finite human mind. To attain the presence of God's inner essence would necessitate that either God descend from the absolutely perfect and sanctified realm of His existence to the lower, less sanctified realm of His creatures, or that the creatures ascend to God's realm of absolute existence. Both of these would negate Divine Oneness. God cannot lower His rank to equal that of His mortal creatures and still remain Almighty God.

Also, in the Bahá'í view, God is present everywhere. Ascribing temporal or physical limitations to Him, such as closeness or remoteness, is not appropriate. Therefore, references in various scriptures to attaining the presence of God or having a vision of God in the next world must be interpreted as achieving the presence of God's representative – the manifestation or prophet who will continue to act as humanity's guide in the next world:

> The one true God is in Himself exalted beyond and above proximity and remoteness. His reality transcendeth such limitations. His relationship to His creatures knoweth no degrees. That some are near and others are far is to be ascribed to the manifestations themselves.[29]

The Soul's Powers

Bahá'u'lláh teaches that, when in the next world, the soul is not bound by the physical limitations of the body:

> The human soul is exalted above all egress and regress. It is still, and yet it soareth; it moveth, and yet it is still. It is, in itself, a testimony that beareth witness to the existence of a

world that is contingent, as well as to the reality of a world
that hath neither beginning nor end.[30]

In the following passages, He describes the role of advanced souls in
humankind's earthly progress and achievements:

> Know thou, of a truth, that if the soul of man hath walked
> in the ways of God, it will, assuredly, return and be gathered
> to the glory of the Beloved. By the righteousness of God! It
> shall attain a station such as no pen can depict, or tongue
> describe. The soul that hath remained faithful to the Cause
> of God, and stood unwaveringly firm in His Path shall, after
> his ascension, be possessed of such power that all the worlds
> which the Almighty hath created can benefit through him.
> Such a soul provideth, at the bidding of the Ideal King and
> Divine Educator, the pure leaven that leaveneth the world of
> being, and furnisheth the power through which the arts and
> wonders of the world are made manifest.[31]

> The light which these souls radiate is responsible for the
> progress of the world and the advancement of its peoples.[32]

In other passages, 'Abdu'l-Bahá explains how, in the next life, souls will use
newly acquired means and powers to discover previously hidden mysteries:

> Once he [the soul] hath departed this life, he will behold in
> that world whatsoever was hidden from him here: but there
> he will look upon and comprehend all things with his inner
> eye. There will he gaze on his fellows and his peers, and
> those in the ranks above him, and those below.[33]

> The Kingdom is the world of vision where all the concealed
> realities will become disclosed . . . The mysteries of which
> man is heedless in this earthly world, those he will discover
> in the heavenly world, and there will he be informed of the
> secret of the truth.[34]

Experiencing the Afterlife while on Earth

'Abdu'l-Bahá notes that certain individuals may even experience the Kingdom of God while still on earth:

> Those souls that, in this day, enter the divine kingdom and attain everlasting life, although materially dwelling on earth, yet in reality soar in the realm of heaven. Their bodies may linger on earth but their spirits travel in the immensity of space. For as thoughts widen and become illumined, they acquire the power of flight and transport man to the Kingdom of God.[35]

Proper Attitude towards Death

To Bahá'ís, death simply signals the beginning of a new stage in the spiritual education of the soul. In fact, in one passage, Bahá'u'lláh calls death a "messenger of joy":

> O Son of the Supreme!
> I have made death a messenger of joy to thee. Wherefore dost thou grieve? I made the light to shed on thee its splendor. Why dost thou veil thyself therefrom?[36]

When asked about the proper attitude toward death, 'Abdu'l-Bahá replied:

> How does one look forward to the goal of any journey? With hope and with expectation. It is even so with the end of this earthly journey. In the next world, man will find himself freed from many of the disabilities under which he now suffers.[37]

GENERAL ESCHATOLOGY

Bahá'í general eschatology is markedly similar to the Christian Fourth Gospel. Perhaps the only notable point of disagreement between the two is how humanity achieves 'salvation.' Both Bahá'u'lláh and the author of the Fourth Gospel propose spiritual interpretations for many dramatic events of the last days. For example, the Fourth Gospel proclaims that Jesus Christ *was* the judgment for humankind. Bahá'u'lláh not only confirms this but claims that *He* is the judgment for today's humanity. Those who accept His revelation gain salvation and those who knowingly reject Him are among the lost. In fact, according to Bahá'u'lláh, every time a new prophet or manifestation has appeared, He has been the judgment for the people of His time. The notion of a physical resurrection in which all the dead are raised from their graves to account for their deeds is not taken literally in the Bahá'í writings.

Bahá'u'lláh explains that the language used in various scriptures of the past to refer to the major events of the last days is mainly figurative. Events such as the blasts of the trumpet by angels to announce the arrival of the Day of Judgment, the raising of the dead, the setting up of the balances to weigh people's deeds, and the souls' crossing of the bridge all have spiritual connotations. To take such events literally and to expect them to happen under apocalyptic or cataclysmic circumstances in a near or distant future is not considered feasible.

Bahá'u'lláh defined these descriptions as metaphors used by past manifestations of God to depict significant spiritual events associated with the coming of the next manifestation. In other words, prophets used a language that was comprehensible to the people of their time.

Bahá'í Interpretations of Apocalyptic Events

A pivotal notion in the general eschatology of many religions is that, at an unspecified time in a distant future, the world will literally come to an end, and all people who have ever lived will be raised from the dead, undergo a final judgment, and receive due recompense for their earthly deeds. But to Bahá'ís, as we have seen, every time a manifestation of God has appeared, His advent has constituted the Day of Judgment for the people of His time. Those who knew of Him, chose to accept Him, and followed His teachings gained the heaven of His goodwill. Those who chose to reject Him remained in error and were subject to God's wrath. The trumpet blast spoken of in the Bible and the Qur'án signifies the call of the new messenger from God, which awakens humankind from the slumber of ignorance. Resurrection is the time when the spiritually dead accept the new manifestation of God and are resurrected from the tomb of unbelief and ignorance.

In this context, terms such as birth and death signify spiritual birth and death. Matthew 8: 22 supports this. Here, Christ is reported to have said to a young man who wanted to delay his acceptance of Christ's message long enough to bury his father: "Let the dead bury the dead." Or, let those who are spiritually dead (those who knowingly rejected Him) bury the physically dead. Corporeal resurrection is not accepted by Bahá'u'lláh. His writings clearly state that, once decomposed, no physical entity, including the human body, will ever be recomposed into its previous form. Thus, the term resurrection can only have *spiritual* significance:

> By the terms "life" and "death" spoken of in the scriptures, is intended the life of faith and the death of unbelief. The generality of the people, owing to their failure to grasp the meaning of these words, rejected and despised the person of the Manifestation, deprived themselves of the light of His divine guidance, and refused to follow the example of that immortal Beauty.[38]

> Even as Jesus said: "Ye must be born again" [John 3: 7]. Again He saith: "Except a man be born of water and of the Spirit, he cannot enter into the Kingdom of God. That which is born of the flesh is flesh; and that which is born of the Spirit is spirit" [John 3: 5–6]. The purport of these words is that whosoever in every dispensation is born of the Spirit and is quickened by the breath of the Manifestation of Holiness, he verily is of those that have attained unto "life" and "resurrection" and have entered into the "paradise" of the love of God. And whosoever is not of them, is condemned to "death" and "deprivation," to the "fire" of unbelief, and to the "wrath" of God.[39]

The balance or scales is the new book of God brought by the prophet of the age. Its contents are the surest means for the salvation and happiness of humanity for that period. Souls are judged based on their acceptance or rejection of this book. Bahá'u'lláh explains:

106

> Say: O leaders of religion! Weigh not the Book of God with
> such standards and sciences as are current amongst you, for
> the Book itself is the unerring balance established amongst
> men. In this most perfect balance whatsoever the people
> and kindreds of the earth possess must be weighed, while
> the measure of its weight should be tested according to its
> own standard, did ye but know it.[40]

The bridge in Zoroastrian and Islamic eschatology, which stretches over hell and leads to heaven, signifies the message of God sent down through His prophet. Whoever accepts this message will enter the heaven of God's goodwill. Those who choose to reject it may fall into the hell of His wrath.

The establishment of the Kingdom of God on earth as it is in heaven is equated by Bahá'ís with the conscious and willed establishment of a new, global civilization based on spiritual principles as envisioned by Bahá'u'lláh. The establishing of this new world order is to take place in three successive phases. The first phase is marked by social breakdowns and widespread suffering for the generality of humankind. This suffering results from humanity's rejection of God's message for this age:

> We have a fixed time for you, O people! If ye fail, at the
> appointed hour, to turn towards God, He, verily, will lay
> violent hold on you, and will cause grievous afflictions to
> assail you from every direction. How severe indeed is the
> chastisement with which your Lord will then chastise you.[41]

In the second phase, humanity will achieve what the Bahá'í writings term the 'Lesser Peace.' This phase will witness the signing of a general agreement among the nations of the world to settle their disputes without resorting to war. The Lesser Peace is, thus, a period of *political* peace during which international security measures are taken to prevent the recurrence of war among nations. The nations will consent to this agreement before the end of the current century to attain collective security: "Should any one among you take up arms against another, rise ye all against him, for this is naught but manifest justice."[42]

During this second phase, many basic social ills will persist. Gradually, however, the third phase will begin, during which Bahá'u'lláh's message will be embraced by most people, and humankind will be united into a single large family. A global civilization will emerge and the 'Most Great Peace' will be established. These events will usher in the golden age of humanity and bring to fruition the past prophecies regarding the establishment of God's kingdom on earth as it is in heaven. 'Abdu'l-Bahá describes it as follows:

> All nations and kindreds will become a single nation.
> Religious and sectarian antagonism, the hostility of races
> and peoples, and differences among nations, will be elimi
> nated. All men will adhere to one religion, will have one
> common faith, will be blended into one race, and become a
> single people. All will dwell in one common fatherland,
> which is the planet itself.[43]

Perhaps the most significant contribution of Bahá'í eschatology lies in its rejection of literal interpretations of afterlife concepts. Bahá'í writings offer symbolic interpretations for such notions as heaven and hell; the Bahá'í heaven is not a physical place but a spiritual state of proximity to God's manifestation. Similarly, the Bahá'í hell is not a place of physical torture but a spiritual state of deprivation from God's bounties. This shift in perspectives means that Bahá'í beliefs about the purpose of this life and the nature of the next life are radically different from those of most other religions. For example, for most Christians the purpose of life is salvation by grace through belief in Jesus, so that through a leap of faith the individual will, upon death, enter into an eternal state of celestial stasis. The Bahá'í writings see life as an eternal challenge to achieve spiritual growth – a process that begins on earth and continues for eternity:

> The Bahá'í concept envisions salvation as motion itself, the
> profound joy of being in motion toward godliness. Human
> satisfaction or fulfillment does not, therefore, await some
> future point of achievement, any more than gaining knowl
> edge awaits a finished point of understanding before learn-

ing brings rewards. The process of learning is itself enjoyable and always relative . . .

In short, the human soul in motion has achieved its fundamental objective. Its long-term goal is to sustain that progress . . . From such a perspective, life in heaven as it is often portrayed by the teachings of other religions – a physical place of comfort and ease – would seem to be an experience quickly doomed to utter boredom. A truly heavenly condition would more likely involve an endless progression of fulfillment and enlightenment.[44]

NOTES

1. *Encyclopedia Britannica, 1992 Britannica Book of the Year*, p. 269

2. Bahá'u'lláh, *Gleanings from the Writings of Bahá'u'lláh*, pp. 156–57

3. 'Abdu'l-Bahá, *Paris Talks*, pp. 90–91

4. W. S. Hatcher. and J. D. Martin, *The Bahá'í Faith: The Emerging Global Religion*, p. 100

5. Bahá'u'lláh, *Tablets of Bahá'u'lláh*, p. 156

6. Bahá'u'lláh, *Gleanings*, p. 287

7. Ibid., p. 68

8. Ibid., p. 149

9. 'Abdu'l-Bahá, *Promulgation of Universal Peace*, p. 226

10. Bahá'u'lláh, *Gleanings*, pp. 155–56

11. J. E. Esslemont, *Bahá'u'lláh and the New Era*, pp. 193–94

12. 'Abdu'l-Bahá, *Some Answered Questions*, pp. 230–32

13. Bahá'u'lláh, *Gleanings*, pp. 170–71

14. Ibid., p. 171

15. Esslemont, p. 194

16. 'Abdu'l-Bahá, *Some Answered Questions*, p. 224–25

17. Bahá'u'lláh, *Gleanings*, p. 154

18. Ibid., pp. 156–57

19. Ibid., p. 345

20. Ibid., p. 156

21. Ibid., p. 157

22. Esslemont, p. 190

23. 'Abdu'l-Bahá, *Bahá'í World Faith: Selected Writings of Bahá'u'lláh and 'Abdu'l-Bahá*, p. 367

24. Bahá'u'lláh, *Gleanings*, p. 156

25. 'Abdu'l-Bahá, *Bahá'í World Faith*, p. 367

26. 'Abdu'l-Bahá, *Selections from the Writings of 'Abdu'l-Bahá*, pp. 193, 195

27. Bahá'u'lláh, *Gleanings*, p. 170

28. 'Abdu'l-Bahá, *Some Answered Questions*, p. 243

29. Bahá'u'lláh, *Gleanings*, pp. 185–86

30. Ibid., pp. 161–62

31. Ibid., p. 161

32. Ibid., p. 157

33. 'Abdu'l-Bahá, *Selections*, p. 171

34. 'Abdu'l-Bahá, *Bahá'í World Faith*, p. 367

35. 'Abdu'l-Bahá, *Selections*, p. 202

36. Bahá'u'lláh, *The Hidden Words of Bahá'u'lláh*, p. 25

37. 'Abdu'l-Bahá, *'Abdu'l-Bahá in London*, p. 96

38. Bahá'u'lláh, *The Book of Certitude*, p. 114

39. Ibid., p. 118

40. Bahá'u'lláh, *The Kitab-i-Aqdas*, p. 56

41. Bahá'u'lláh, *Gleanings*, p. 214

42. Ibid., p. 254

43.'Abdu'l-Bahá quoted in Shoghi Effendi, *The Promised Day is Come*, p. 117

44. J. S. Hatcher, *The Purpose of Physical Reality: The Kingdom of Names*, p. 56

GLOSSARY

'Abdu'l-Bahá: 'Servant of Glory.' The eldest son of Bahá'u'lláh and His successor.

Bahá'í: A follower of Bahá'u'lláh.

Bahá'u'lláh: 'Glory of God.' The prophet-founder of the Bahá'í Faith.

Lesser Peace: The global *political* peace that the Bahá'ís believe will come about out of necessity for collective security before the close of this century.

Most Great Peace: The *spiritual*, lasting peace that will follow the political or Lesser Peace.

Progressive Revelation: The belief that religious truth, much like scientific truth, is relative, and that throughout history humankind has received guidance from various prophets that is appropriate to its spiritual, intellectual and socio-cultural capacity.

World Order of Bahá'u'lláh: Bahá'í equivalent of the Christians' Kingdom of God on earth, which will usher in the golden age of humanity.

CHAPTER 8
REINCARNATION
& TRANSMIGRATION

INTRODUCTION

The origin of belief in transmigration and the related notion of reincarnation has been lost over time. Reincarnation has come to mean rebirth into another body of the same species, particularly human. Transmigration is a broader term, usually indicating a passage across the boundaries of all forms of existence: plant, animal, human, demonic, and divine. While most people today associate the doctrine of transmigration of souls with Indian thought in general and with Hinduism and Buddhism in particular, the extant evidence does not seem to point to a particular region of the earth or a specific culture as the cradle for this belief. The idea might well be as ancient as the human race and may have co-existed in different parts of the ancient world before ideological exchange among previously isolated peoples became more prevalent. Documented practices of many primitive cultures in different parts of the globe confirm widespread belief in the passage of one's soul, or vital essence, into the bodies of newly-born humans or other life forms. For instance, some archaeologists argue that the reason the people of the New Stone Age (c. 10,000 to c. 5,000 BCE) placed the corpses of their dead in the fetal position at burial was to facilitate their rebirth. This is reinforced by the ancient human practice of washing the dead, perhaps to cleanse them magically and prepare them for rebirth.[1] Today, belief in reincarnation and transmigration of souls is as vigorous as ever in many parts of the world. Different groups in Africa, Asia, the Pacific Ocean, Australia, the Americas, and Europe accept transmigration as fact.

Throughout Africa many tribes have believed in reincarnation for centuries. The Zulus' creed includes a sophisticated system of reincarnation: an immortal soul contains in itself the spark of the divine universal spirit – the I Tongo – and humans exist in a hierarchy of seven grades. After many rebirths, the noblest of humans in the seventh grade reach a state of release from rebirth. They dwell on earth in any physical form they wish and can maintain or relinquish that form at any time. The final destiny of all humans is reunion with the I Tongo.[2]

In the Pacific Ocean, the Papuans and other inhabitants of New Guinea refuse to eat fish, pig, or cassowaries because they believe these animals are animated by the spirits of their dead. When dying, the inhabitants of the Lifu and Solomon Islands in the Pacific tell their families which creatures their souls will inhabit so that their relatives will never kill or injure these creatures.[3] The tribes of the northern clan of central Australia also believes in the transmigration of souls – all living people are viewed as reappearances of the dead. Like some African tribes, many Australian tribes hold that, upon death, their souls linger in the vicinity to find a woman into whose womb they may pass for rebirth.[4]

Many Indian tribes in the Americas also believe in reincarnation. For instance, some Hurons of eastern Canada believe in two souls – one remains in the cemetery following physical death until relatives hold a feast for the dead, when this soul will go down to the underworld; the other soul stays close to the decaying corpse until it is born again in a descendant. Hurons also buried their children by the roadside to let their souls enter into the wombs of passing women.[5]

IMMORTALITY

To understand the concept of transmigration, it is necessary to examine it within the larger context of such related topics as immortality, the make-up of the human soul or the remaining substance in humankind, and a system of retribution for one's deeds based on the justice of a Creator God. An extensive treatment of these subjects, however, is outside the scope of this book. Nevertheless, a brief examination of the notion of immortality is essential since, by definition, transmigration presupposes the idea of an immortal substance in humans. Immortality cannot of course be proved or disproved by pure reason, and the basis or origin of the belief in immortality among humans is not entirely clear. Some assert that personal immortality may simply be a universal human desire. Others have postulated that the belief may be based on a superstition rooted in human dreams or natural experiences.

Evidence from anthropologists shows that belief in a life after death was widespread among early cultures. In contrast to the ethical world-views of most religious systems through the ages, many early cultures, including the Babylonian and Assyrian, saw no relation between conduct on earth and the nature of the life beyond. The ancient Egyptians, how-ever, believed in an afterlife shaped by earthly conduct. There were three likely scenarios for the dead Egyptian – unification with a god, transmi-gration into an animal for a lifetime, or voluntary metamorphosis into another life form for one's own benefit.[6] The practice of embalming the dead and furnishing them with food, utensils, and expensive jewelry pro-vides clear evidence of Egyptian belief in an afterlife. In all likelihood, however, Egyptians borrowed the belief in human survival after death from the Aryans of either Persia or India with whom they had come into contact. The followers of the ancient Persian prophet Zoroaster believed in the survival of the human soul after death which, based on earthly con-duct, would end up in an eternal heavenly or hellish environment. The Aryan and perhaps even the pre-Aryan indigenous inhabitants of India, on the other hand, believed that after death the human soul would "pass into the trunks of trees or the bodies of animals, but especially into the bodies of birds, reptiles, and insects."[7]

TRANSMIGRATION IN EASTERN THOUGHT

The doctrine of the transmigration of souls has been nurtured in Indian thought for several millennia, and underlies the belief systems of most Indian religions including Hinduism, Buddhism, and Jainism. As noted in Chapter 1, the ancient Vedic period (c. 1,500 BCE) provides no evidence for this doctrine. According to the Vedas, righteous souls were destined to enjoy eternal life in a heaven of blissful joys and tangible pleasures, while the souls of the wicked were doomed to sink into the abyss of an eternal hell. In the second period of Indian literature (850–500 BCE), however, the Vedic notion of immortality as existence in an eternal heaven or hell sud-denly gave way to a belief in countless earthly existences in different life forms.

The earliest work that established the foundation of this belief was the *Satapatha Brahmana* or "the Brahmana of the hundred ways." Brahmanas were Vedic commentaries written by various Hindu sages. The introduction of this principle of transmigration in the *Satapatha Brahmana*, so suddenly and without apparent transitional stages, has baffled many scholars. One theory is that the authors of this particular Brahmana and the later Upanishads borrowed this notion from the general Indian folklore prevalent among the Aryan people of the Indian peninsula who, as noted, believed in the passing of human souls into a variety of different life forms.

The doctrine of transmigration outlined in the *Satapatha Brahmana* appears fully developed. At the root of this work's argument is the hypothesis that there is no unmerited happiness or misery in human life. What happens to us in our present life is the direct consequence of our deeds in a past life. From this supposition, it is argued that the same principle should hold true for our previous lives, *ad infinitum*. These premises give rise to several corollary theories: if the human soul or vital essence is pre-existent, it must be immortal too, and as there is no unmerited happiness or misery, justice requires that this immortal substance go through endless existences in various life forms according to the merits of its deeds; in addition, a pre-existent, eternal universe is also needed within which the transmigration of these souls can take place.

Naturally, belief in transmigration of the soul quickly removed the need for the Vedic notion of a single eternal heaven and a single eternal hell. These were supplanted by belief in endless existences in various life forms. The only way to release oneself from continuous deaths and rebirths was to come to a special knowledge, the knowledge of Brahman, the soul of the universe, and realize that Brahman was the only true existence. Everything else we observed in the phenomenal world was illusory. Once souls came to this knowledge, especially to the realization of the identity of their individual souls (*atmans*) with the Brahman, they would be released from continuous rebirths.

Unlike Hinduism, Buddhism appears to teach neither the existence of a human soul nor its transmigration. What most Buddhists insist on is rather the revolution or stream of existences. At death, a substance they call "the germ of consciousness" is passed on to a new fetus in a mother's womb. The nature of the life of the new person depends on the quality of the potencies contained in the germ. A popular Buddhist metaphor for this process is the lighting of a new candle from one burned out. The only thing remaining from the first candle is the flame.

This surviving germ of consciousness can be defined as a "life-craving set of character dispositions and latent memories which become attached to a new embryo to form a fresh empirical self."[8] As noted in the chapter on Buddhism, human rebirths can take place in any of six different realms. The three upper realms are reserved for the righteous, the three lower for the wicked. None of these conditions are, however, eternal. The Buddha Himself is said to have been reborn into every life form to help the liberation of all creatures from the bondage of rebirth. The Buddhist Jatakas (birth stories) chronicle some 550 narratives of Buddha's births in various life forms. Thus, according to popular Buddhist belief, "there is not a particle of earth anywhere which the Buddha has not sanctified by some form of existence on or in it."[9]

The purpose of life for a Buddhist is liberation from continuous rebirths. This is only possible by releasing oneself from the bondage of all *karma* – good or evil. Buddha also taught the existence of a collective *karma* for humanity made up of the *karma* of different societies and cultures. The goal of all existences is to extinguish all *karma* and achieve nirvana. Nirvana is full enlightenment and complete passionlessness. It is freedom from all desires and attachments that cause suffering and sorrow. Nonetheless, despite the obvious contradiction, the Buddha does not appear to rule out completely the western idea of a life of bliss for the righteous and a life of suffering for the evil-doer in another higher world. There are several passages attributed to the Buddha which seem to confirm the western version of an afterlife. For instance, in the *Dhammapada* (vv. 17–18), the Buddha attempts to impress on the minds of His followers the existence and significance of a higher world: "A man whose words are lies, who transgresses the Great Law [*Dharma*], and who scorns the higher world – there is no evil this man may not do." In another passage, the Buddha distinguishes between "this world" and "the next" and seems to hint at the western idea of a single heaven (the good place) for the righteous and a single hell (the evil place) for the evil-doer:

He [the evil-doer] sorrows in this world, and he sorrows in the next world: the man who does evil sorrows in both worlds. "I have done evil," thus he laments, and more he laments on the path of sorrow. He [the righteous] rejoices in this world, and he rejoices in the next world: the man who does good rejoices in both worlds. "I have done good," and thus he rejoices on the path of joy.

TRANSMIGRATION IN WESTERN THOUGHT

Among the earliest references to transmigration in western thought are those found in the Orphic writings of sixth century BCE, attributed to Orpheus, a legendary figure in ancient Greece. Both Plato (427–347 BCE) and Aristotle (384–322 BCE) recognized Orpheus as the author of a set of sacred books which deal with a wide range of subjects, including theogony, purification, and the afterlife, and Plato's great myths of the Republic, Phaedo, and Phaedrus show obvious Orphic influence. The philosophic brotherhood of Pythagoras (582–500 BCE) was also decidedly Orphic. Orphic poems even found their way in the writings of Neoplatonists, including the great Plotinus (205–270 CE) as well as the lesser thinkers of that group. Some Orphic literature on eschatology, written on thin plates of gold, were later discovered buried in graves in southern Italy.

The Orphic genesis states that humankind came into being from the soot generated by the burning bodies of the Titans slain by Zeus – the supreme deity of the ancient Greeks – after the Titans had killed and eaten Zeus' son Zagreus. From this tragedy, humanity inherited a small divine element – Zagreus – and a large evil Titanic element. The purpose of human life is to eliminate the Titanic element so that human beings can rise to divine status.

Orphic eschatology asserts that the human soul is a divine essence shut up in the tomb or prison of the body. This essence survives bodily death and receives afterlife retribution for earthly conduct, but is later reincarnated in a human or animal body to continue what certain Orphic documents call the "wheel" or "circle" (cyclos).[10] The ultimate goal of human life is release from this weary wheel or circle of reincarnations and the achievement of divine status. Successive reincarnations are seen as a period of purgation and this period can be shortened by living the "Orphic" life. The great Greek philosopher and statesman Empedocles not only subscribed to these Orphic teachings but vigorously taught them. He recalled memories of his reincarnations as a youth, a maiden, a bush, and a fish. Like his predecessor Pythagoras, Empedocles also prohibited the eating of flesh and killing of animals and stigmatized these acts as the shedding of kindred blood.[11]

Early esoteric Jewish literature only tolerated transmigration. Philo (30 BCE–40 CE), the most important representative of Hellenistic Judaism, seems implicitly to approve of the doctrine of transmigration. He viewed humanity as captive to sensual desires which, without assistance from above, can never rise to true virtue and wisdom. To him, the purpose of human life was to try to liberate oneself from the body of sense and facilitate the return of the soul to its original divine condition. The human soul came from God and must rise to Him again. However, natural death brings this liberation only to those who live saintly lives of detachment from things of the senses. The natural consequence of this teaching seems to be that the vast majority of humans would at death pass into other bodies to continue to work on their detachment in future lives.

If Philo appears ambivalent on transmigration, the Jewish Kabbala is quite clear in its support of this doctrine. Kabbalistic writings are very explicit in accepting transmigration as punishment for the sins of previous existences. Such punishments fit the crime. Thus, if someone had sinned with his or her eyes, that person would be born blind in the next earthly life, and, similarly, every other part of the body would be affected by the nature of the sin committed. The later Kabbalistic writings completely embraced transmigration and extended future rebirths to the realms of animals, plants, stones, and metals. Most Kabbalists believe that no soul migrates through more than three bodies but others support a greater number of migrations. Kabbalists have drawn up extensive spiritual genealogies which include lists and books that recount the reincarnations of righteous and wicked people of bygone ages.[12]

In Christian circles, certain Gnostic sects of the first centuries as well as the Manichaeans of the fourth and fifth centuries embraced transmigration, while in the Middle Ages, numerous Christian sects collectively known as the Cathari also subscribed to this belief.[13] During the Renaissance, the Italian philosopher Bruno (1548–1600) promoted it and later the German poet and novelist Goethe (1749–1832) toyed with the idea. However, most orthodox Christians have vigorously opposed it through the ages.

CONCLUSION

In general, western religions reject the possibility of transmigration. They usually confirm a single earthly existence followed by death and retribution for earthly conduct. For instance, Hebrews 9: 27 states that "Man is destined to die once, and after that to face judgment." Christian eschatology teaches that after death a human being's vital essence or soul assumes a "spiritual" or "glorified" body and continues to exist. The Bahá'í Faith also suggests that, after separation from the body, the human soul will take on a new form appropriate for its new habitation. There is no mention of transmigration in the sacred literature of Zoroastrianism or Islam.

For the major western religions, transmigration puts too much emphasis on humanity's physical existence on earth and lessens the significance of its primarily spiritual nature. Western religions view humans as the only species with the gift of an indivisible, indestructible, rational soul, which can ponder the hidden mysteries of the universe, build civilizations, and come to know and worship its creator. All other life forms on earth are seen as devoid of these capacities, and these religions see no historical evidence to suggest that these uniquely human characteristics have ever transmigrated to any other form of life on earth.

However, while these religions remain largely skeptical of the validity of transmigration or its value as a theory or doctrine, there is little doubt that some sectors of humanity have benefitted from belief in transmigration. Perhaps the most significant contribution of this doctrine has been the promotion of an ethical worldview rooted in the belief in an afterlife shaped by earthly conduct, associated with the need to acquire divine knowledge and an understanding of the true nature of the soul in order to secure release from continuous deaths and rebirths. In addition, this doctrine has been instrumental in the development in its adherents of an affection for all life forms, including animals and plants.

To the surprise of many westerners, transmigration has also promoted the highly advanced notion of a systems view of the universe. All existences are seen as a single integrated system of interconnected beings and processes that, to different degrees, affect each other's well-being. Belief in transmigration, incorporating as it does the promise or possibility of a better life to come, has also served as a support system for many of its followers through the ages. For those suffering under oppressive circumstances, a belief in transmigration has provided a vehicle for sustaining the hope of a better future for themselves and their children.

While, on the surface, the eastern and western religions may seem to be at complete odds in regard to the doctrine of transmigration, they do seem to agree on the central issue: What is the purpose of life? Both confirm that individuals are to follow a spiritual, rather than a material, path in life. They see the sanctification of one's character and its freedom from worldly desires as major goals. Therefore, while the means prescribed by eastern and western religions for achieving these spiritual goals may be irreconcilable, their ends appear to be identical.

NOTES

1. D. Christie-Murray, *Reincarnations: Ancient Beliefs and Modern Evidence*, p. 16

2. Ibid., pp. 17–18

3. Ibid., p. 22

4. Ibid., pp. 23–24

5. Ibid., p. 26

6. J. Hastings (ed.), Encyclopaedia of Religion and Ethics, vol. 12, p. 431

7. Ibid., p. 434

8. Christie-Murray, p. 42

9. Ibid., p. 43

10. *Encyclopaedia Britannica*, vol. 15, p. 266

11. Hastings, p. 433

12. Ibid., p. 438

13. *Encyclopaedia Britannica*, p. 266

CHAPTER 9
THE NEAR-DEATH EXPERIENCE (NDE)

Recent advances in emergency health care have resulted in a rapidly growing number of people being rescued from the verge of death. Often, these individuals report out-of-body experiences during which they have feelings of pure joy and peace and undergo memorable encounters, hold telepathic communions with beings of light, and experience instantaneous, panoramic reviews of their earthly lives. The frequency and similarity of these reports have intrigued a number of physicians and psychologists, and some have been spurred into investigating this phenomenon, known as the near-death experience or NDE.

Dr. Raymond Moody, a philosopher and a psychiatrist, is probably the best-known contemporary investigator of NDEs. His popular books *Life After Life* and *Reflections on Life After Life* were two of the first published studies. Moody interviewed numerous individuals during his research. They fell into one of two broad categories:

1. Those who were resuscitated after they were pronounced clinically dead.

2. Those who, through severe injuries or illnesses, came very close to death.[1]

In his first book, Moody gives the overall impression that the afterlife experience is uniformly blissful. The recollections of many of his subjects are so pleasurable and exhilarating that they are often at a loss for words to describe what they went through. For many, the experience was so overwhelming and spiritually uplifting that they did not want to return to their earthly lives. In his second book, however, Moody provides not only positive NDEs but several different kinds of afterlife experiences. One example is the unpleasant "limbo" mode of experience remembered by a number of individuals who felt they were paying penalties for breaking certain "rules" while on earth. This included people who had attempted suicide.

In a positive NDE, the person finds himself in a realm of peace, joy, and love. This realm is inhabited by an awesome, but loving, being of light who surrounds the subject with love and warmth, and provides a breathtaking, spectacularly beautiful replay of the person's life on earth. Other radiant, all-knowing beings also populate this realm and communicate perfectly with each other in a telepathic manner.

Sometimes, the intensity of a positive NDE is remarkable. Cultural anthropologist Patrick Gallagher was comatose for several weeks following a near-fatal car accident in 1976. During this time, he had a series of vivid, stunning NDEs:

> Not only was I freed from gravity but from all other human restrictions as well. I could fly, and fly so adeptly that I felt transformed . . . Next in sequence was the sight of a dark area ahead, void of all light, which I saw to be the entrance of a tunnel . . . Finally I saw a circular light in the distance . . . of yellow-orange color of total beauty . . .
>
> When I left the tunnel, I entered a dazzlingly beautiful area . . . It was complete space, that is . . . totally and perfectly illuminated . . . I saw [there] a number of people, some of whom were clothed and some of whom weren't. The clothing, which seemed transparent, was adornment but not . . . shielding . . .
>
> The people themselves [were] also of graceful beauty . . . Everyone there, as I knew the very moment I was there, seemed to possess a knowledge as radiant, transfiguring and ideal as the luminous light. And I possessed it, too . . . I knew that all one had to do was approach an interesting person and quite easily and almost immediately *understand his essence*. To do so completely, required only a brief glance . . . into the person's eyes, without any speech . . . the result was [a] consummate exchange of knowledge. Words cannot provide a hint of such universal knowledge.

Without reflection or words, I knew them as completely as they knew me, and finally understood why poets cite eyes as the entrance to the soul . . . I also knew that the illuminating light would never cease: no one had the need to sleep . . . I also understood that everyone present was in a state of perfect compassion with everyone else and everything else . . . We were freed from all those contrivances historians claim to be the cause of war and other conflicts, including land, food, and shelter. Love was the only axiom. These ideal conditions produced a phenomenal state, for neither hate nor any other disturbing passion was present – only the total presence of love . . .

I knew it was quite possible to return to my terrestrial life, and I missed . . . my children, my wife, and many others. I did decide to return, though I knew that the price of the ticket would be gargantuan: accepting the biological, physiological, and physical needs and handicaps of my body, as well as the loss of all but a splinter of my luminous knowledge. I know nothing of any aspect of the return trip, but as soon as I decided to return and so lost the ALL of what I have ever wanted to be or to know, I was there.[2]

Literally millions of people around the globe from all walks of life have recollected similar positive and negative experiences. In North America alone, an estimated five per cent of the population have had an NDE.[3] Atheists are as likely to have NDEs as the devoutly religious. Their positive accounts, too, contain a tunnel, a being of light, and so on.

However, the individual's cultural or religious background does seem to have an impact on how he or she interprets the experience. For instance, while a Christian may describe the being of light as Jesus, a Muslim may identify Him as Alláh (God). In nearly all instances, an NDE leaves an indelible mark on the person's life, and frequently the response is a prompt and radical reorientation of one's value system. Kenneth Ring, another prominent investigator of NDEs, surveyed 26 individuals who had NDEs and evaluated possible changes in their attitudes and value systems. In his book, *Heading toward Omega*, he draws the following conclusion:

After NDEs, individuals tend to show greater appreciation for life and more concern and love for their fellow humans while their interest in personal status and material possessions wanes. Most people with NDEs (NDEers) also state that they live afterward with a heightened sense of spiritual purpose and, in some cases, that they seek a deeper understanding of life's essential meaning. Furthermore, these self-reports tend to be corroborated by others in a position to observe the behavior of NDEers.[4]

CHARACTERISTICS OF NDEs

In his most recent book, *The Light Beyond*, Moody identifies nine characteristics of a typical near-death experience.[5] These are:

A Sense of Being Dead
Many people who begin to experience an NDE after a cardiac arrest are confused and frightened at first because they don't know what is happening to them. Often they find themselves floating above their bodies and wonder why, all of a sudden, they can see their bodies from a distance. Gradually they begin to understand what is happening and try to get the attention of those who are tending them or attempting resuscitation, but to no avail. A woman resuscitated by Moody himself later told him how she had tried to stop him because she was enjoying the experience; but when she tried to grab Moody's arm, her hand had passed right through it.

When attempts to communicate with others fail, the NDEer often begins to experience an increased sense of self-identity; he begins to feel his uniqueness. Factors such as family ties take a backseat to the person discovering his inner self. One woman described this as "a cutting of ribbons."[6] Just as a balloon is freed when its strings are cut, many NDEers have a sense of freedom from earthly limitations and can experience their true self in its totality; fear frequently turns to utter joy at this point.

Peace and Painlessness
Before the "ribbons" are cut, the sick or injured person often experiences

severe pain, but this is soon replaced with intense pleasure and total peace.

Out-of-Body Experience

Next, the person feels himself rising up and begins to get a view of his body below. Separated from his physical body, he now sees himself in a spiritual body. Most NDEers are at a loss to describe this new body; some say it is an energy field, others a cloud of colors. One NDEer told Moody he closely examined his hands and found them to be composed of tiny structures of light.

The Tunnel Experience

Shortly after the out-of-body experience, the person begins to realize that he may be dying. A tunnel or portal appears to him and he feels propelled toward this tunnel and into the darkness. At the end of the tunnel there is a bright light.

People of Light

Beings of light, who are glowing with awesome luminescence, come to meet the person at the end of the tunnel, and fill him with love. Some NDEers have described the light emanating from these beings as the purest form of love. Despite its intensity, this light is not painful to the eyes but warm and vibrant. These people of light are often deceased relatives or friends of the NDEer, and they begin to communicate with him telepathically. There is immediate and complete understanding.

The Being of Light

Shortly thereafter, the NDEer feels the presence of a spectacular being of light. Depending on the subject's religious or ethical convictions, he may identify this holy being as God, Christ, Buddha or another holy figure. This being, who radiates total love and understanding, appears to atheists and agnostics as well as the religious.

The Life-Review

As the NDEer is basking in the warmth and love of this glorious being of light, there passes before him a three-dimensional, panoramic review of every single event in his lifetime. Curiously, time as we know it is not a factor in this review. The person's whole life is suddenly laid bare before him, and he gets a chance to comprehend the effects of all of his actions upon various people in his earthly life. By penetrating other people's consciousness, the NDEer can now personally feel the joy, happiness and pleasure, or conversely, the despair, pain, or distress that his actions brought upon others.

Throughout this review, the being of light stays with the subject and helps him learn from his mistakes. The review helps the NDEer understand that the two most important provisions he needs for the next life are love and knowledge; in almost every case, individuals who have had NDEs become much more loving and detached, and they develop an unquenchable thirst for knowledge.

Rising Rapidly through the Heavens

While most people who have NDEs experience passing through the tunnel, some describe a "floating experience" in which they rapidly rise into heaven. The renowned psychotherapist Carl Jung had such an experience during a heart attack in 1944. Others have recounted similar episodes where they see themselves rising above the earth or zooming upward and seeing the planets around them.

Reluctance to Return

Many near-death experiences are so breathtaking that the people who have them often do not want to come back to their normal lives. Some become angry and even rebuke their doctors for bringing them back. Others feel that the being of light gives them a choice. Those who do want to come back to life often have selfless motives such as concern for the families they are leaving behind. Others may have different reasons. Moody relates the extraordinary case of a woman who had two NDEs about 30 years apart:

> One woman in Los Angeles has faced this question [of wanting to go back] from the Being of Light twice in her life. Once in the late fifties when she was in a coma following an automobile accident, the Being told her it was time to die and go to heaven. She argued with him, complaining that she was too

young to die. But the Being wouldn't budge until she said, "But I'm young, I haven't danced enough yet." At that point, the Being gave out a hearty laugh and allowed her to live.

About thirty years later, she had a cardiac arrest while undergoing minor surgery. Again she passed through the tunnel and found herself with the Being, and again he told her it was her time to die. This time she argued that she had children to raise and couldn't leave them at this point in their lives. "Okay," said the Being. "But this is the last time. The next time you have to stay."[7]

ARTISTS' INTERPRETATIONS

A number of artists appear to have had NDEs themselves or have illustrated other people's accounts of such experiences. A well-known example is the *Ascent into the Empyrean* by the sixteenth-century Dutch painter Hieronymus Bosch (see Illustration 9). In this painting, we see both the tunnel and the light at the end of the tunnel, and in the lower foreground angels can be seen attempting to guide the deceased upward toward it. As the dead go through the tunnel, they enter the presence of a magnificent being of light, and reverently kneel in this light as it engulfs them. This is also illustrated by Gustave Doré in a well-known engraving of Dante and Beatrice (see Illustration 10).

Dante Alighieri (1265–1321) was the author of *La Divina Commedia*, generally considered to be the greatest literary work in the Italian language and one that had a great impact on Christian views about heaven and hell. In this epic poem of three major divisions, Dante explains his imaginary journey through hell and then to the mountain of purgatory, where souls struggle to learn virtue. From there, Beatrice – Dante's personification of other-worldly enlightenment – takes him through nine heavens and into the spaceless Empyrean. Here, Dante is allowed a brief glance of God Himself:

> Forth from the last corporeal are we come
> Into the Heaven, that is unbodied light;
> Light intellectual, replete with love;
> Love of true happiness, replete with joy;
> Joy, that transcends all sweetness of delight.[8]

Dante's vision of God as unbodied light has a Zoroastrian flavor. His depiction of paradise typifies medieval images of heaven as an otherworldly garden of delight filled with fountains, sweet-songed birds, fruit-laden trees, and pavilions decked with various kinds of flowers, crystals and jewels.

HISTORICAL PARALLELS

Although until recently NDEs were not widely known or investigated, the experience is perhaps as old as humanity itself. The earliest written accounts of NDEs are over 2,500 years old. The writings of Plato, one of the greatest thinkers of all time, include references to NDEs; like his teacher Socrates, Plato was a highly spiritual man. Descriptions of death and the life of the soul after separation from the body abound in his works, and many of the elements of contemporary NDEs can be found there.

For example, *The Republic* contains the story of a Greek soldier named Er who, following a close brush with death, describes what he saw in the realms beyond earthly life. After his soul separates from his body, Er joins a group of other spirits and, using "openings" or "passageways," they all travel away from the earth into the realms of the afterlife. There, the other souls with him are judged by divine beings who can see, at a glance, all the deeds each soul has performed in his earthly life. But Er is not judged because his time has not yet come. He is told by the judges that he should go back to earth to inform its inhabitants of what the realms of the afterlife are like.

Another early account of an NDE can be found in the *Dialogues*, a set of spiritual writings composed by the sixth-century pope, Gregory the Great. The final book of *Dialogues* contains 42 stories in support of the soul's immortality. One such tale is the story of a soldier who almost dies but returns to give a dramatic account of the afterlife and also of the fate of a merchant from Constantinople named Stephen:

> A certain soldier in this city of ours happened to be struck down (by a plague). He was drawn out of his body and lay lifeless, but he soon returned and described what befell him.

At that time there were many people experiencing these things. He said that there was a bridge, under which ran a black, gloomy river which breathed forth an intolerable foul-smelling vapor. But across the bridge there were delightful meadows carpeted with green grass and sweet-smelling flowers. The meadows seemed to be meeting places for people clothed in white. Such a pleasant odor filled the air that the sweet smell by itself was enough to satisfy [all the needs of] the inhabitants who were strolling there. In that place each one had his own separate dwelling, filled with magnificent light . . .

On the bridge, there was a test. If any unjust person wished to cross, he slipped and fell into the dark and stinking water. But the just, who were not blocked by guilt, freely and easily made their way across to the region of delight . . . On the same bridge, he claimed to have recognized that Stephen of whom we spoke before. In his attempt to cross the bridge, Stephen's foot slipped, and the lower half of his body was now dangling off the bridge. Some hideous men came up from the river and grabbed him by the hips to pull him down. At the same time, some very splendid men dressed in white began to pull him up by the arms. While the struggle went on, with good spirits pulling him up and evil spirits dragging him down, the one who was watching all this was sent back to his body. So he never learned the outcome of the struggle.[9]

Gregory's account recalls the ancient Zoroastrian and Hindu descriptions of the afterlife (see Chapters 1 and 2).

ALTERNATIVE THEORIES

While those who have experienced NDEs, as well as most NDE investigators such as Raymond Moody and Kenneth Ring, are convinced of the validity and the metaphysical nature of these experiences, many scientists and medical professionals have proposed alternative theories and explanations for them. These range from describing them as manifestations of mental illness to blaming temporary chemical imbalances in the brain or the release of endorphins in the brain; other ascribed causes include the effects of drugs and anaesthetics, temporal lobe seizure, and even conscious fabrication.

NDEs as Manifestations of Mental Illness

Many medical professionals have dismissed NDEs or its individual elements such as the out-of-body experience as manifestations of various types of mental illness. These range from schizophrenic symptoms such as hallucinations, delusions, and loose associations to organic mental disorders such as delirium. To their dismay, many NDEers who have attempted to share their positive and uplifting experience with doctors have been told to ignore or forget it. Some doctors have even referred NDEers to psychotherapists and mental hospitals. This may partially explain why, until recently, many NDEers have been reluctant to share their experience with others, including family and friends.

But are NDEs really a form of mental illness? Let's look at the schizophrenic symptoms that some in medical circles believe are involved in NDEs.

Visual Hallucination: seeing people or objects that don't really exist.
Auditory Hallucination: hearing voices that aren't there.
Delusions: false beliefs; for instance, an individual may become absolutely convinced that he is Alexander the Great.
Loose Associations: someone who has difficulty organizing his or her thoughts and keeps jumping from one unrelated subject to another during conversation is said to suffer from this symptom.[10]

People exhibiting schizophrenic symptoms are often tormented by what they see or hear, or by their inability to hold their thoughts together. Eventually, their situation worsens, and many become severely depressed. Others become incapable of functioning in society and are institutionalized. In contrast, the attitudes and social functioning of NDEers are frequently much improved after their experience. Although as part of their experience most NDEers have seen a being of light, none have identified themselves with Napoleon or God because of it.[11] In addition, unlike schizophrenic episodes that are incoherent and recurring, NDEs are always coherent and happen once or very few times in a person's lifetime.

NDEs are Due to Chemical Imbalances

Some people in the field of medicine have dismissed NDEs as delirium, a symptom of an acute chemical imbalance in the brain which is typically reversible and does not entail permanent brain damage. Most NDEs occur in conditions when the brain is temporarily deprived of oxygen and can react in peculiar ways. Moody explains that delirious experiences are always disorienting and impair the person's awareness of his or her surroundings; delirious people also have frequent nightmarish hallucinations, typically involving animals or insects. They show little coherence in their thought patterns and have difficulty concentrating. After a delirious episode, the patient can only vaguely remember its details.

None of these factors is associated with NDEs. No one with delirium has described the episode as having a deep personal meaning or a spiritually transformational effect on his or her life; and none of the common NDE features such as the out-of-body experience, the tunnel, the being of light, or the life-review are cited in reports of delirious episodes. While delirium is often described as a 'bad trip,' most NDEs are considered spiritual turning points in the lives of those who experience them.[12]

Out-of-Body Experiences (OBEs) as Autoscopic Hallucinations

Moody writes that some medical practitioners claim that OBEs are autoscopic hallucinations. This is a fascinating phenomenon which is not widely known, although it has been reported by many individuals throughout history. During an autoscopic hallucination, a person sees a completely convincing projection of his own image in front of him, as he might see any other person close by. Individuals suffering from migraine headaches and epilepsy often experience such mental self-projections. Moody mentions that US President Abraham Lincoln once reported such an experience. While lying on a sofa in the White House, Lincoln related, he saw a full-length image of himself as if looking in a mirror. Aristotle also describes an Athenian who frequently saw himself walking among the crowds in the streets of Athens.

While many individuals have reported such hallucinations, in

Moody's view there are obvious differences between these and out-of-body experiences. For example, the center of awareness of the person with an OBE lies outside his physical body, while the individual undergoing an autoscopic hallucination is experiencing the projection of an image from inside his own physical body. Also, the projected body that the person with an autoscopic hallucination sees is solid as it is in life, whereas the body that someone with an OBE sees is always transparent. Moreover, unlike OBEers who are frequently able to travel to other places without their physical bodies and give precise accounts of what happened there, those with autoscopic hallucinations cannot and do not report such incidents because they are experiencing the hallucination from inside their physical bodies.[13]

The Tunnel Experience as a Leftover Memory from the Birth Experience
Carl Sagan, the noted American scientist and astronomer, has suggested that the tunnel experience in NDEs is nothing more than a memory of the experience of birth. As Moody notes, on the surface this comparison makes sense, because we all have similar birth experiences where we struggle through the birth canal and are eventually pulled into a colorful and bright world by people who are glad to see us. Here is Sagan describing his theory:

> The only alternative, so far as I can see, is that every human being, without exception, has already shared an experience like that of those travelers who return from the land of death: the sensation of flight; the emergence from darkness into light; an experience in which, at least sometimes, a heroic figure can be dimly perceived, bathed in radiance and glory. There is only one common experience that matches this description. It is called birth.[14]

Sagan's theory appears plausible until one examines the research that is available on the capabilities of newborn babies. Moody cites the following from Carl Becker, a philosophy professor at Southern Illinois University who examined pediatric research to find out how much of the birth experience newborns can understand and retain. Among Becker's findings were that there are extensive studies of infant perception amply demonstrating that at birth the human mind is not yet well enough developed to perceive or remember much of anything. Sagan's suggestion that the beings of light who greet the NDEer are recollections of the midwife, doctor, or the father who greeted the newborn when he or she emerged from the birth canal, therefore, seems dubious. Infants show no response to light, unless the contrast between light and darkness is at least 70 percent; they cannot focus on an object. Newborns have rapid and disorganized eye movements, particularly when they are crying, which is what most newborns do. Tears further blur infants' vision. Half of all newborns can't even focus on an object at arm's length, let alone perceive and remember it. During the first month, no infant is capable of fully focusing on an object five feet away.

In addition to Becker's arguments, Moody suggests that, because infants' perceptions are not well developed at birth and they have almost no experience with shapes and patterns, they cannot logically be expected to make sense of what they experience during birth. Even if they had the capacity to perceive and remember things, they would still not be able to see much because, during the actual birth, the face is pressed against the walls of the birth canal. Furthermore, the birth experience is often a traumatic one for the infant during which he or she is "turned upside down, spanked, and cut with scissors to sever the umbilical cord."[15] If an NDE is simply the reliving of the memory of birth, it should often be a negative, painful experience, not a positive and spiritually transforming one.

NDEs as Universally Available Mystical Experiences

Other noted investigators of NDEs have proposed that these and similar supernatural phenomena, such as heavenly visions of prophets, mystics, and saints, are all members of a family of related mystical experiences. Richard Heinberg suggests such mystical experiences are potentially available to everyone, because we all seem to have a certain consciousness of the realm beyond. Even if Heinberg is correct, such visions must be more readily available to the spiritually inclined and to the select few in history who have claimed access to divine revelation and forever changed the course of human history.

Heinberg proposes that our intense desire to attain paradise or heaven might be due to some buried memory – both individual and collective – of a happier time in the past when human beings lived in a paradisal environment much like the home of Adam and Eve before their fall.

The Zoroastrian *fravashi* belief also emphasizes that heaven is the true and lasting plane of existence for humanity. According to this doctrine, a person's spirit remains in heaven even during his or her physical life on earth. The Zoroastrian creation myth notes that when God created the physical world, all *fravashi*s (spirits) were consulted to see if they chose to take on physical forms and participate in the battle with evil, or remain in purely spiritual forms and, thus, stay out of the conflict. The *fravashi*s collectively chose to take on material forms.[16] The strong human desire for attaining paradise or heaven while still on earth might thus be explained as an innate need to return to one's true plane of existence (paradise) in one's higher form (immortal spirit).

ARE NDEs TRULY UNIQUE SPIRITUAL EXPERIENCES?

None of the current medical and psychological explanations can adequately explain the NDE phenomenon. That NDEs are universally available mystical experiences cannot, of course, be easily proved or disproved, but given the nature of NDEs and their life-transforming impact, this may be the most plausible explanation yet.

The NDE element that is most difficult for scientists and medical professionals to dismiss is the out-of-body experience. There is currently no scientific explanation of how individuals claiming OBEs are able to give such detailed accounts of what various medical staff said and did during their resuscitation. Even more puzzling are the amazingly accurate accounts of OBEers who have been able to describe what was happening elsewhere while their physical bodies were lying in a hospital's operating room. To Moody and most NDE investigators, the only reasonable ex-planation is that such experiences are genuine. For example, there seem to be no other explanations for these two accounts cited by Moody:

A forty-nine-year-old man had a heart attack so severe that

after thirty-five minutes of vigorous resuscitation efforts, the doctor gave up and begin filling out the death certificate. Then someone noticed a flicker of life, so the doctor continued his work with the paddles and breathing equipment and was able to restart the man's heart.

The next day, when he was more coherent, the patient was able to describe in great detail what went on in the emergency room. This surprised the doctor. But what astonished him even more was the patient's vivid description of the emergency room nurse who hurried into the room to assist the doctor. He described her perfectly, right down to her wedge hairdo and her last name, Hawkes. He said that she rolled this cart down the hall with a machine that had what looked like two Ping-Pong paddles on it (an electro-shocker that is basic resuscitation equipment).

When the doctor asked him how he knew the nurse's name and what she had been doing during his heart attack, he said that he had left his body and – while walking down the hall to see his wife – passed right through nurse Hawkes. He read the name tag as he went through her, and remembered it so he could thank her later.

I talked to the doctor at great length about this case. He was quite rattled by it. Being there, he said, was the only way the man could have recounted this with such complete accuracy.

On Long Island, a seventy-year-old woman who had been blind since the age of eighteen was able to describe in vivid detail what was happening around her as doctors resuscitated her after a heart attack.

Not only could she describe what the instruments used looked like, but she could even describe their colors.

The most amazing thing about this to me was that most of these instruments weren't even thought of over fifty years ago when she could last see. On top of all this, she was even able to tell the doctor that he was wearing a blue suit when he began the resuscitation.[17]

In the absence of substantiated alternative explanations for such cases and their subsequent impact on people's lives, NDE investigators including Moody propose that NDEs are real spiritual events allowing us a glimpse into the next world.

NOTES

1. A. R. Moody, Jr., *Life After Life: The Investigation of a Phenomenon – Survival of Bodily Death*, p. 16

2. P. Gallagher, "Over Easy: A Cultural Anthropologist's Near-Death Experience," pp. 140–49

3. R. Heinberg, *Memories and Visions of Paradise*, p. 230

4. K. Ring, *Heading toward Omega*, p. 141

5. A. R. Moody, Jr. with P. Perry, *The Light Beyond*, pp. 5–12

6. Ibid., p. 7

7. Ibid., p. 13

8. A. Dante, *The Divine Comedy*, p. 413

9. Moody, *The Light Beyond*, pp. 82–83

10. Ibid., p. 89

11. Ibid., p. 90

12. Ibid., pp. 95–96

13. Ibid., pp. 97–98

14. Ibid., p. 137

15. Ibid., p. 139

16. J. R. Hinnells (ed.), *The Facts on File Dictionary of Religions*, p. 127

17. Moody, *The Light Beyond*, p. 13

CHAPTER 10
RELIGION &
THE NDE
PHENOMENON

I n the previous chapter, we said that many scientists and medical professionals have dismissed NDEs and proposed alternative hypotheses for this mysterious phenomenon, but there is currently no substantial body of evidence to support any of these views. The paranormal nature of NDEs prevents medical specialists from duplicating them in a laboratory setting, so most scientists will no doubt continue to be skeptical of the view that NDEs indicate the existence of a life after death.

One prevalent scientific theory defines human consciousness as a product of electromechanical processes in the brain. According to this theory, when the brain dies, so does consciousness and life. However, the theory has not been proved, and a series of studies by neurosurgeon Wilder Penfield failed to link human consciousness to the brain's electromechanical processes. Hence, late in his career, Penfield concluded that the human mind or consciousness must be an independent entity separate from the physical brain.[1] It is conceivable, therefore, that reductionist science may continue to have difficulty providing rational explanations for NDEs, as such phenomena may prove to be primarily metaphysical and thus lie outside the realm of science.

CAN RELIGION PROVIDE ANY ANSWERS?

One area to which we might look for some answers to the NDE puzzle is religion. Unlike minimalist science, traditional religion takes a maximalist view of reality by recognizing the validity of metaphysical experiences. Religion not only allows for the perception of reality through means other than the senses, it considers knowledge gained through the physical senses to be valuable but potentially limiting. Religious teachers remind us that we are being fooled by our senses all the time. For instance, we take mirages to be real water, and we can't see things at a distance that eagles can see or hear sounds that dogs can hear. If our physical senses are so imperfect, how can we expect the knowledge we gain through them to be complete? To obtain a holistic view of reality, therefore, we should supplement scientific knowledge with revelatory knowledge given to us in the scriptures.

SCRIPTURAL PARALLELS

Most religious people probably have little difficulty accepting NDEs as paranormal yet real events, because such episodes can confirm their belief in an afterlife. A fundamental principle of most religious systems is faith in the survival of a non-material substance or entity that conquers death. This substance has been labeled among other things, as soul, spirit, mind, or consciousness. Without this cornerstone, religion cannot establish belief in a system of reward and punishment, which is its chief instrument in attempting to influence human conduct. Thus, it should come as no surprise that all the great living religions talk about this imperishable substance and the nature of its life after it separates from the physical body.

But do the various scriptures support the picture that those who have had NDEs depict for us of the realms beyond? Interestingly, close examination of the religious literature of various faiths reveals striking parallels between religious and NDE accounts of the afterlife. Perhaps some of the most astonishing parallels are those found in the Tibetan Book of the Dead (*Bardo Thodol*). This text was probably authored by the founder of Tibetan Buddhism, and it provides irrefutable evidence that the various components of NDEs which we find so intriguing today were already well known to ancient Tibetans. However, this book is not a description of the *eternal* heavens and hells that other scriptures talk of; it is mostly an account of the various experiences the human soul supposedly goes through in the bardo state between reincarnations. This intermediate state is said to last 49 days.

The author of the Book of the Dead notes that, after death, the soul first lingers around the body for a few days (which is similar to certain Zoroastrian accounts) and that during and after this stage, the soul experiences three intermediate states. In the first state, it will have visions of a being of clear light in a magnificent landscape. When encountering this light, the soul is advised to sever all attachments to its former personality and identify itself with the light. If it fails to do so, the soul will proceed to the second intermediate state. Here, it will assume a psychically projected body that resembles its former physical body, and shortly thereafter find itself in the presence of seven divine beings. If it cannot identify with any of these beings, the soul will then encounter seven terrifying demons, and be told that it should acknowledge these grotesque beings as projections of its own subconscious and watch them without fear. In the third and last state, the soul is empowered to move about the physical world instantaneously and without any effort. It observes its relatives mourning and attempts, in vain, to convince them it is still alive. For a while, it wanders aimlessly in sorrow until it finds itself in the presence of the Lord of the Otherworld – Yama, the king and judge of the dead. This majestic being orchestrates a review of the soul's life on earth so it can feel "the torture of the demons of its own fears and desires."[2]

Survival of a Non-Material Entity

We said that certain scriptures of almost all religions acknowledge the survival of an imperishable entity or substance which conquers death and has afterlife experiences. Most scriptures appear to agree with NDE accounts that this entity is not made up of matter. In fact, some writings argue that it is the non-material nature of the soul that guarantees its immortality. After the separation from the body, the soul survives and assumes a form "that best befitteth its immortality and is worthy of its celestial habitation."[3] Below are three NDE accounts that support this view of the nature of the soul:

> I remember being wheeled into the operating room and the next few hours were the critical period. During that time, I kept getting in and out of my physical body, and I could see it from directly above. But, while I did, I was still in a body – not a physical body, but something I can best describe as an energy pattern. If I had to put it into words, I would say that it was transparent, a spiritual as opposed to a material being. Yet, it definitely had different parts.[4]

> I was out of my body looking at it from about ten yards away,
> but I was still thinking, just like in physical life. And *where* I
> was thinking was about at my normal bodily height. I wasn't
> in a body as such. I could feel something, some kind of a –
> like a capsule, or something, like a clear form. I couldn't
> really see it; it was like it was transparent, but not really. It
> was like I was just there – an energy, maybe, sort of like just
> a little ball of energy. And I really wasn't aware of any bodi-
> ly sensation – temperature, or anything like that.[5]

> He was there but he didn't have a physical body. It was kind
> of like a clear body, and I could sense every part of it –
> arms, legs, and so on – but I wasn't *seeing* it physically.[6]

The Being of Light

The majority of individuals with NDEs recollect the presence of a kind,
loving being of pure light. They find this encounter so remarkable that
they often feel unable to describe it well:

> It [the being of light] did seem that it was a little dim at
> first, but then it was this huge beam. It was just a tremen-
> dous amount of light, nothing like a big bright flash light, it
> was just too much light. And it gave off heat to me; I felt a
> warm sensation. It was a bright yellowish white – more
> white. It was tremendously bright; I just can't describe it. It
> seemed to cover everything, yet it didn't prevent me from
> seeing everything around me . . . From the moment the light
> spoke to me, I felt really good – secure and loved. The love
> which came from it is just unimaginable, indescribable.[7]

Most scriptures acknowledge that, in the afterlife, the soul of the deceased
will at some point have an encounter with a great being. In many cases, as
in Zoroastrianism, Christianity, and Islam, this being is identical with
God. In Zoroastrianism, the righteous soul's encounter with God is considered to be the greatest joy of heaven. God (Ahuramazd), described as
a non-human entity, will appear to the soul in the form of pure light. In

the following passage, the author of the Book of Viraf, who has traveled throughout various hells and finally reached heaven, describes his experience with God (the Beauteous Vision): "And when Ahuramazd spoke in this manner, I remained astonished, for I saw a light, but I saw nobody; I also heard a voice, and I understood that 'This is Ahuramazd.'"[8]

For Christians, the supreme reward of righteous souls is the unimpeded sight of God in heaven (I Corinthians 13:21; Revelation 22:4). Islam also speaks of the "Vision of God" in paradise as the greatest joy awaiting the faithful: "Upon that day faces shall be radiant, gazing upon their Lord" (75: 22). However, if taken literally, this verse would raise a serious dilemma for Muslim theology: how can the absolutely transcendent God of Islam (Alláh) make Himself appear to His creatures in paradise without compromising His transcendence?

In other scriptures, the being of light is equated not with God but with other holy beings. For instance, in many strands of Hinduism and Buddhism, the great being in the afterlife is considered to be Yama, the first man to die and now the king and judge of the dead.

In the Bahá'í Faith, the great being is the Holy Spirit or the divine nature of the manifestation (prophet or intermediary between God and man), as God's transcendence precludes the possibility of directly experiencing Him in any realm of existence. Bahá'u'lláh identifies God's essence or innermost being as the one and only form of absolute existence. A face-to-face encounter with God would require either that He descend from His absolutely sanctified realm to the lower realms of His own creatures, or that the soul could ascend to God's realm. Either of these would negate God's uniqueness and put Him on a par with His own creatures. So, as God and His creatures can never meet in the same realm, the encounter must be with His most perfect creation – the manifestation – who is in a form we can better understand and relate to. Just as our physical bodies could not survive closeness to the sun, our souls are not capable of surviving or experiencing a personal encounter with the creator.

Life-Review

Another frequently reported component of both positive and negative NDEs is the vivid, instantaneous review of one's earthly life in the presence of the being of light. In positive NDEs, this review is panoramic and unspeakably glorious:

> When the light appeared, the first thing he said to me was
> "What do you have to show me that you've done with your
> life?", or something to this effect. And that's when these
> flashbacks started . . . Now, I didn't actually see the light as I
> was going through the flashbacks. He disappeared as soon
> as he asked me what I had done, and the flashbacks started,
> and yet I knew that he was there with me the whole time,
> that he carried me back through the flashbacks, because I
> felt his presence, and because he made comments here and
> there. He was trying to show me something in each one of
> these flashbacks. It's not like he was trying to see what I had
> done – he knew already.[9]

Conversely, in negative NDEs, the review is gloomy, even terrifying, as in
the case of individuals who have attempted suicide. Moody cites the
example of a man who had shot himself following the death of his wife
and was resuscitated. He remembered the following: "I didn't go where
[my wife] was. I went to an awful place . . . I immediately saw the mistake
I had made . . . I thought, 'I wish I hadn't done it.'"[10]

Other people who had tried to commit suicide also told Moody of
this same horrible place. Many of them felt they would remain there for a
long time as a penalty for attempting "to release themselves prematurely
from what was, in effect, an 'assignment' – to fulfill a certain purpose in
life."[11]

From the religious perspective, the pleasant and unpleasant recollections of different NDEers might be viewed as desired evidence for the
existence of a system of divine retribution in the afterlife. The religious
mind would interpret NDEs as glimpses of the divine judgment awaiting
a particular soul. The joy, peace, and love experienced by some NDEers
could be considered as indications of the positive judgment awaiting
those with fruitful earthly lives, while the horrors witnessed by other
NDEers who had 'broken rules' could be regarded as the negative judgment awaiting them in the afterlife.

The life-review component of NDEs is hinted at in a number of religious scriptures, but the majority of these mention only negative life-reviews for the sinful. The Tibetan Book of the Dead and the Zoroastrian Datastan-i-Denik fall into this category; according to these sources, shortly after death the wicked will undergo very frightening reviews that depict the sins and crimes committed during earthly life. However, there is no specific denial in either of these sources that there is also a panoramic review for the righteous. The emphasis on the horrible experiences awaiting the wicked in these sources might simply be an attempt to persuade the ungodly to change their ways.

As mentioned above, in many schools of Hinduism and Buddhism, Yama judges the dead. In Zoroastrianism, of course, the judge is either Zoroaster Himself or Mithra and his two assistants; in Christianity, the judgment is rendered by either Christ or, in some instances, God; in Islam, the judge is always Alláh (God); while in the Bahá'í Faith, the divine aspect of the manifestation (Holy Spirit, the Word) renders the judgment. A number of passages in Bahá'í scripture mention the existence of a divine judgment for each soul:

> Bring thyself to account each day ere thou art summoned to
> a reckoning; for death, unheralded, shall come upon thee
> and thou shalt be called to give account for thy deeds.[12]
> It is clear and evident that all men shall, after their physical
> death, estimate the worth of their deeds, and realize all that
> their hands have wrought.[13]

Meeting Others

Often, NDEs include encounters with other souls, particularly those of relatives and friends:

> They were all people I had known in my past life, but who
> had passed on before. I recognized my grandmother and a
> girl I had known when I was in school, and many other rela-
> tives and friends . . . They all seemed pleased. It was a very
> happy occasion, and I felt that they had come to protect or
> to guide me. It was almost as if I were coming home, and
> they were there to greet or to welcome me.[14]

Another man remembered:

> Several weeks before I nearly died, a good friend of mine,
> Bob, had been killed. Now the moment I got out of my
> body I had the feeling that Bob was standing there, right
> next to me. I could see him in my mind and felt like he was
> there, but it was strange. I didn't see him as his physical
> body. [15]

While the scriptures of most religions suggest that heaven or paradise is the abode of all the righteous where the inhabitants can meet and recognize their relatives and friends, certain passages in the Bahá'í writings clearly refer to this:

> As to the question whether the souls will recognize each other
> in the spiritual world: This fact is certain; for the Kingdom is
> the world of vision where all the concealed realities will
> become disclosed. How much more the well-known souls will
> become manifest . . . how much more will he recognize or dis-
> cover persons with whom he hath been associated. [16]

DISCREPANCIES BETWEEN NDEs AND RELIGIOUS ACCOUNTS

The most obvious discrepancy between religious writings and the accounts of those who have had near-death experiences lies in their descriptions of heaven and hell and the kinds of pleasures and pains that await us in the afterlife. Generally, positive NDE accounts include descriptions of a realm approximating the religious concept of heaven. The inhabitants of this realm are a loving, all-knowing being of light and other people of light who live an eternal, utopian life of utter joy, peace, and love. These beings have spiritual or celestial bodies which are transparent and glow with light.

While certain writings in most religions suggest the non-material nature of our immortal soul or spirit, the vast majority of these works portray heaven as a physical place not only of joy, peace, and love but of fulfillment of one's earthly wishes and desires. The nature of the earthly pleasures promised seems to depend on the intellectual and cultural receptivity of the early believers. For instance, earthly pleasures mentioned in the Islamic paradise are tailored to the needs and desires of the typical Bedouin of the Arabian desert lands, so the righteous Muslim is promised unlimited supplies of water, honey, and milk. Certain Muslim traditions extend these simple pleasures and also promise scope for hedonistic patterns of sexual behavior and the excessive drinking of wine. Similar hedonism is also promised and sanctioned in certain Buddhist texts. None of the sensuality of these representations of heaven is, however, noted in any NDE account.

Another discrepancy is in the reported duration of heavenly existence. Most NDEers with positive experiences have related that they felt they had begun an eternal life in an eternal realm, which resonates with most religious accounts. However, certain Hindu and Buddhist texts speak of a hierarchy of *transitory* heavens between reincarnations, where the righteous receive temporary rewards in proportion to their good deeds. No NDEer has so far corroborated this. NDE reports of spiritual rewards in a timeless, placeless mode of existence are to some extent echoed in Bahá'í writings. Yet the Bahá'í claim for the existence of countless spiritual realms – and an invisible hierarchy of souls where the less advanced are unable fully to appreciate the station of the more spiritual souls – is not easily verifiable through NDE accounts.

The other major distinction between NDE and religious accounts is in descriptions of the abode of the wicked or misguided. Those who have had unpleasant NDE experiences describe a horrible place or state of existence in the afterlife, and some of these individuals, such as those who had tried to commit suicide, felt they would remain there for a long time. However, there is no mention of the traditional hell of fire and brimstone in unpleasant near-death experiences. Instead, the afterlife torments in NDEs have a positive outcome. They usually consist of the gaining of some sort of knowledge, resulting in the subject's growth; for example, knowledge of why suicide or certain other actions are undesirable, or of how a cruel person's victims have suffered, physically or emotionally. But the detailed, often gruesome, accounts of different kinds of physical punishments found in many religious texts have no parallel in NDE accounts.

The tangible representations of hell in religious literature, however, may have been an attempt by prophets to customize their descriptions to the particular fears of their contemporaries. Bahá'í writings argue that there is a relationship between humanity's level of understanding and the degree of sophistication of the religious message conveyed in different epochs: "Know of a certainty that in every Dispensation [religion] the light of Divine Revelation hath been vouchsafed unto men in direct proportion to their spiritual capacity."[17] In another passage, Bahá'u'lláh explains why the message should always be tailored to the capacity of the hearer:

> Follow thou the way of thy Lord, and say not that which
> the ears cannot bear to hear, for such speech is like luscious
> food given to small children. However palatable, rare and
> rich the food may be, it cannot be assimilated by the diges-
> tive organs of a suckling child.[18]

Despite the apparent differences in the descriptions used in sacred scrip-tres to convey the state and condition of the human soul after death, it can be argued that what many of them have in common is that they essential-ly evoke the same kind of response in the followers of the different tradi-tions. Whether heaven and hell are represented in primarily physical and sensual terms, or are spiritually depicted, teachings about the afterlife invariably reinforce for the believer the importance of following a spiritu-al path in this physical world.

Scriptural evidence indicates that the founders of various religious systems have often resorted to parables and symbolic language to make their message more meaningful and relevant to the understanding, desires, and fears of their hearers. As a kind parent would speak the language of a child in order to explain an important point, the prophets have each used a language that is relevant, vivid, and understandable to their followers.

NOTES

1. R. Heinberg, *Memories and Visions of Paradise*, p. 231

2. Ibid., pp. 232–33

3. Bahá'u'lláh, *Gleanings from the Writings of Bahá'u'lláh*, p. 157

4. A. R. Moody, Jr., *Life After Life: The Investigation of A Phenomenon – Survival of Bodily Death*, p. 47

5. Ibid., p. 48

6. Ibid., p. 54

7. Ibid., pp. 60–61

8. M. Haug & E. W. West, *The Book of Arda Viraf*, p. 203

9. Moody, pp. 62–64

10. Ibid., p. 136

11. J. S. Hatcher, "Afterlife and the Twin Pillars of Education," in *World Order*, p. 28

12. Bahá'u'lláh, *The Hidden Words of Bahá'u'lláh*, p. 25

13. Bahá'u'lláh, *Gleanings*, p. 171

14. Moody, p. 53

15. Ibid.

16. 'Abdu'l-Bahá, *Bahá'í World Faith: Selected Writings of Bahá'u'lláh and 'Abdu'l-Bahá*, p. 367

17. Bahá'u'lláh, *Gleanings*, p. 87

18. Bahá'u'lláh, *The Gift of Teaching*, p. 13

BIBLIOGRAPHY

'Abdu'l-Bahá. *Selections from the Writings of 'Abdu'l-Bahá*, Haifa, Bahá'í World Center, 1978

—. *Paris Talks: Addresses given by 'Abdu'l-Bahá in Paris in 1911–12*, 11th ed., London, Bahá'í Publishing Trust, 1979

—. *Some Answered Questions*, comp. and trans. Laura Clifford Barney, rev. ed., Wilmette, Illinois, Bahá'í Publishing Trust, 1981

—. *'Abdu'l-Bahá in London*, London, Bahá'í Publishing Trust, 1982

—. *Promulgation of Universal Peace*, Wilmette, Illinois, Bahá'í Publishing Trust, 1982

Bahá'í World Faith: Selected Writings of Bahá'u'lláh and 'Abdu'l-Bahá, Wilmette, Illinois, Bahá'í Publishing Trust, 1976

Bahá'u'lláh. *Tablets of Bahá'u'lláh*, trans. H. Taherzadeh, Haifa, Bahá'í World Center, 1978

—. *The Book of Certitude*, Wilmette, Illinois, Bahá'í Publishing Trust, 1983

—. *Gleanings from the Writings of Bahá'u'lláh*, trans. S. Effendi, 2nd rev. ed., Wilmette, Illinois, Bahá'í Publishing Trust, 1983

—. *The Hidden Words of Bahá'u'lláh*, Oxford, Oneworld Publications, 1986

—. *The Kitab-i-Aqdas*, Haifa, Bahá'í World Center, 1992

Bleeker, C. J. and G. Widengren. *Historia Religionum*, Leiden, E. J. Brill, 1969

Charles, R. H. *Eschatology: The Doctrine of a Future Life in Israel: Judaism and Christianity*, New York, Schocken Books, 1963

Christie-Murray, D. *Reincarnations: Ancient Beliefs and Modern Evidence*, Sturminster Newton, Dorset, Prism Unity, 1988

Clasenapp, H. V. *Immortality and Salvation in Indian Religions*, Calcutta, Susil Gupta India Ltd., 1963

Conze, E. *Buddhist Scriptures*, London, Penguin Books, Ltd., 1959

Dante. *The Divine Comedy*, trans. H. F. Carey, New York, Doubleday & Company, Inc., 1947

Dewick, E. C. *Primitive Christian Eschatology*, Cambridge, Cambridge University Press, 1912

Encyclopedia Britannica. 1992 Britannica Book of the Year, Chicago, Encyclopedia Britannica, Inc., 1992

Esslemont, J. E. *Bahá'u'lláh and the New Era*, Wilmette, Illinois, Bahá'í Publishing Trust, 1980

Ferm, V. (ed.) *An Encyclopedia of Religion*, New York, The Philosophical Library, 1945

BIBLIOGRAPHY

Fozdar, J. *Buddha Maitrya-Amitabha Has Appeared*, New Delhi, Indraprastha Press, 1976

Gallagher, P. "Over Easy: A Cultural Anthropologist's Near-Death Experience," *Anabiosis* 2 (2), 1982

Gift of Teaching, The, London, Bahá'í Publishing Trust, 1977

Griffith, R. T. H. (trans.) *The Hymns of the Rig Veda*, New Delhi, Motilal Banarsidass, 1973

Hamilton, A. (ed.) *Encyclopedia Britannica*, vol. 4, Chicago, William Benton Publisher, 1972

Hastings, J. (ed.) *Encyclopedia of Religion and Ethics*, vol. 12, Herndon, Virginia, Books International Inc., 1926

Hatcher, J. S. "Afterlife and the Twin Pillars of Education," *World Order*, 1979

—. *The Purpose of Physical Reality: The Kingdom of Names*, Wilmette, Illinois, Bahá'í Publishing Trust, 1987

Hatcher, W. S. and J. D. Martin. *The Bahá'í Faith: The Emerging Global Religion*, San Francisco, Harper & Row, 1984

Haug, M. and E. W. West. *The Book of Arda Viraf*, Amsterdam, Oriental Press, 1971

Heinberg, R. *Memories and Visions of Paradise*, Los Angeles, Jeremy P. Tarcher, Inc., 1989

Hellaby, M. *Death the Messenger of Joy*, London, Bahá'í Publishing Trust, 1980

Hinnells, J. R. (ed.) *The Facts on File Dictionary of Religions*, New York, Facts on File, Inc., 1984

Hopkins, T. *The Hindu Religious Tradition*, Encino, California, Dickenson Publishing Company, Inc., 1971

Hughes, T. P. *Dictionary of Islam*, Delhi, Oriental Publishers, 1973

Hume, R. E. *The Thirteen Principal Upanishads*, Madras, Oxford University Press, 1971

Jeffry, A. *Muhammad & His Religion*, New York, The Liberal Arts Press, 1958

Johnson, C. J. and M. G. McGee. *Encounters With Eternity: Religious Views of Death and Life After Death*, New York, Philosophical Library, 1986

Kashyap, B. J. (gen. ed.) *Majjhima-nikaya*, Bihar, Pali Publication Board, 1958

— (gen. ed.) *Khuddaka-nikaya*, Bihar, Pali Publication Board, 1959

Keith, A. B. *The Religion and Philosophy of the Vedas and Upanishads*, vol. 32, Cambridge, Massachusetts, Harvard University Press, 1926

Masse, H. *Islam*, New York, G. P. Putnam's Sons, 1938

McDannell, C. and B. Lang. *Heaven: A History*, New Haven, Yale University Press, 1988

Mehta, P. D. *Early Indian Religious Thought*, London, Luzac & Company Limited, 1956

Moody, A. R., Jr. *Life After Life: The Investigation of a Phenomenon – Survival of Bodily Death*, New York, Bantam-Mockingbird Books, 1975

Moody, A. R. Jr., with Paul Perry. *The Light Beyond*, Toronto, Bantam Books, 1988

Nikhilanada, S. *Essence of Hinduism*, Boston, The Beacon Press, 1948

Noss, D. S. and J. B. Noss. *A History of the World's Religions*, New York, Macmillan Publishing Company, 1990

Noss, J.B. *Man's Religions*, New York, The Macmillan Company, 1949

Pavry, J. D. C. *The Zoroastrian Doctrine of a Future Life: From Death to the Individual Judgment*, New York, Columbia University Press, 1926

Pilcher, C. and D. D. Oxon. *The Hereafter in Jewish and Christian Thought*, London, Society for Promoting Christian Knowledge, 1940

Ring, K. *Heading Toward Omega*, New York, Morrow, 1985

Robinson, R. H. and W. L. Johnson. *The Buddhist Religion: A Historical Introduction* (3rd edition), Belmont, California, Wadsworth Publishing Company, 1982

Salmond, S. D. F. *The Christian Doctrine of Immortality*, London, Morrison & Gibb, 1895

Shoghi Effendi. *The Promised Day is Come*, Wilmette, Illinois, Bahá'í Publishing Trust, 1980

Smith, J. and Y. Haddad. *The Islamic Understanding of Death and Resurrection*, New York, State University of New York Press, 1991

Toynbee, A. et al. *Life After Death*, London, Weidenfeld & Nicolson, 1976

Trenckner, V. (ed.). *Milinda-Panha*, London, William & Norgate, 1880

Werblowsky, R. J. and G. Wigoder. *The Encyclopedia of Jewish Religion*, Jerusalem, Massada P.E.C. Press Ltd, 1966

West, E. W. *The Sacred Books of the East: Pahlavi Texts*, vol. 8, Delhi, Motilal Banarsidass, 1965

Williams, J. *Themes of Islamic Civilization*, Berkeley, University of California Press, 1971

Zaehner, R. C. *The Dawn and Twilight of Zoroastrianism*, New York, G. P. Putnam's Sons, 1961

INDEX